JB JOSSEY-BASS™
A Wiley Brand

Fundraising for Libraries

How to Plan Profitable Special Events

Scott C. Stevenson, Editor

WILEY

978-1-118-69049-9   ISBN

978-1-118-70378-6   ISBN (online)

Fundraising for Libraries:
How to Plan Profitable Special Events

Published by

Stevenson, Inc.

P.O. Box 4528 • Sioux City, Iowa • 51104
Phone 712.239.3010 • Fax 712.239.2166
www.stevensoninc.com

Fundraising for Libraries: How to Plan Profitable Special Events

Table of Contents

Fundraising for Libraries: How to Plan Profitable Special Events

Fundraising for Libraries: How to Plan Profitable Special Events

Selecting the Right Event, Targeting the Right Audience

It was Benjamin Franklin who said, "By failing to prepare, you are preparing to fail." As important as every aspect is of carrying out a successful special event, there is no aspect that is as important as those first planning steps. Selecting the right event for your library, targeting the right audience, timing your event and more all lay the foundation for what is to follow. That's why it's critical that everyone involved in determining special events — that's everyone you hope to have ownership in your event — puts careful thought into it up front.

Learn From Other Libraries' Events

Want to learn how various types of special events work and discover new features that you might want to add to an existing event? Make it your job to attend others' events.

Why not approach other noncompetitive nonprofits in your community or area and come up with a reciprocity agreement: If you can attend their special events for free, they can attend yours.

Having such an agreement in place will allow you to discover more about how a particular event works, and determine if such an event will work for your library as well. And in those instances in which you have the same event, you can discover special features that you may want to incorporate into your event.

"But why would I want to share our events with other nonprofits' event planners? Why would I want them to see how we structure a particular event?" you may ask.

First, there's nothing to prevent others from paying the price of a ticket to attend, so you really have nothing to hide. Second, if you have confidence in your ability to pull off successful, highly attended events, then what do you have to lose?

If you're hesitant, try a reciprocity agreement with a couple of other nonprofits to test your comfort level. Then expand your pool of partners over time.

Take Your Time to Select the Right Fundraising Event

Don't settle on a particular special event simply because someone in your group thinks it would be fun, or you heard it was done successfully at another local library.

By answering the following questions you can select an event that works best for your library and purposes:

- What's the primary objective of your event?
- Does the event under consideration conflict with your library's mission in any way?
- What type of individuals would you like your event to attract and why?
- How important is it that your event reaches out to new individuals — those with no real connection to your library or its work?

- How labor intensive is this event compared to others you may be considering?
- How many volunteers will be required to successfully pull off the event?
- How much planning time will be required?
- What kind of budget will be needed to implement the event?
- How much might you expect to net from the event?
- Do you have existing volunteers/board members familiar with and/or capable of heading up the effort?
- How does the event's timing and potential location measure up?
- How will you ensure maximum attendance for the event?
- How does the anticipated cost of this event compare to other types of events?

Want a New Event?
Try a Brainstorming Session

Before jumping into an event that has you saying "been there, done that," why not take the time to select or create one that is unique to your library?

Assemble a handful of key staff and volunteers — those whom you want to plan and execute the project — for a brainstorming session. Make sure everyone knows that any and all ideas are welcome, no matter how outrageous.

Then allow them to work their magic.

Because those present gave birth to the proposed event, they will own it and want to see it succeed.

Make Space Fit Crowd Size

When planning an event, select a space just large enough for the anticipated crowd.

Too many empty chairs or too few people to fill a room conveys poor attendance. A slightly crowded room, on the other hand, heightens excitement.

For seated events, have slightly fewer chairs set up than expected attendees. Have extra chairs close by as additional numbers of individuals show up.

Testing Your Special Event

While no wave of a magic wand can guarantee special event success, the more work you put into planning, the more likely you'll find the success you seek for your library

One important element of a successful event is a creative, forward-thinking planning committee that can help identify the types of activities your community would be likely to enthusiastically support.

Together, you and your event planning committee should:

❑ **Invite community input.** Start by asking committee members and volunteers for their ideas of a perfect event. Expect diverse answers like golf, walking/running marathons, dressy dances, gourmet dinners, art auctions and celebrity appearances, but take note of preference patterns that may emerge, like swap meet or sudoku tournament. Responses may reveal an activity that has a strong following in your city. Use your website to solicit as many ideas as possible, and list unique suggestions you've received. Add an online poll and see which look like potential winners.

❑ **Evaluate popular existing events.** You don't want to reinvent the wheel, but make a list of galas, lectures, athletic competitions and other fundraisers that always draw crowds. Identify common elements that make these diverse activities successful, including season, venue, chairmen, family-friendly attractions and ticket price.

❑ **Combine proven techniques with a new niche.** You know your venue, committee chairs and menu are winners. Fill a void in the community calendar with a benefit concert, end-of-summer picnic, mid-winter outdoor festival or motivational speaker to combat post-holiday doldrums. Time your event so it won't conflict with summer vacations, holiday parties and youth sports activities.

❑ **Enlist an experienced events consultant.** A professional can help you coordinate the creative activities of the chairman and committee members. A professional can take their ideas and fully develop the event theme while also being able to anticipate potential difficulties and keep timelines on track.

Factors to Consider When Choosing an Event Theme

Whether it's a country-western boot scootin' boogie or a Puttin'-on-the-Ritz gala, consider time of year, logistics and facility when choosing a special event theme. These factors can dramatically affect attendance, ticket price and profits.

For event success:

❑ **Determine formal or casual.** Which best fits your target audience? If your desired crowd relishes the chance to break out the ball gown or tuxedo, choose a theme that lends itself to fine china, lavish floral arrangements and champagne. For those who want to unwind with spicy food and loud music, try enchiladas, margaritas and mariachi bands.

❑ **Fit your ticket price to your theme.** If price per head is $50, think closer to A Night in the Tropics with seafood and mango salsa than Evening in Paris with filet mignon and truffles. Whichever you choose, be sure that the menu will be perceived as appropriate for the admission price, and that the theme won't create unrealistic expectations for the value.

❑ **Choose the right venue.** A marina at the lake on a late spring night works better for a luau event than the grand ballroom at the hotel convention center in December. The jungle habitat at the local zoo may not be the best spot for an early evening cocktail reception while the facility is still open to the public and parking is scarce – even if your theme is Go Wild Wednesday!

❑ **Determine effort involved.** Staging a gala event with a theme usually requires more time and volunteer hours than an Italian-style buffet and local art show. Seating arrangements, centerpieces, table settings and linens are expected for a formal dinner, while a buffet can be self-serve and the art provides the visual interest.

❑ **Consider attire and season.** Themes typically lend themselves to certain types of clothing. Remember that people want to be stylish, appropriate and comfortable. Think of what you would wear to an Oktoberfest beer garden on a fall evening, or to an Oscar Night extravaganza in March. If you have a difficult time reconciling the two, your target crowd probably will, too.

Identify Your Event's Intended Audience

In planning a special event for your library, it's critical you determine just who it is you intend to have as attendees. Without knowing that, you might come up with an event that appeals to no one.

Potential audiences may include, but not be limited to:

- The general public.
- Repeat supporters.
- Corporate guests.
- Small emerging groups.
- A captive audience.

Knowing the characteristics of expected attendees will drive key planning decisions:

- Ticket price.
- Venue, food and decorations.
- Theme, level of formality.
- Entertainment.
- Methods of promotion.
- Items for sale.

Library Event Profile

Library Fundraiser Toasts Different Cultures

It's like taking a trip to another country without having to endure jet lag.

For two years, members of the Shasta Library Foundation (Redding, CA) have organized a culture-themed fundraiser. The Taste of… features thematic décor, authentic food, beverages, entertainment and a silent/live auction. "We wanted a fundraiser that had consistent elements but brought some uniqueness by visiting a different country each year. Our public library supports the event by focusing on programs and displays about the country during the month preceding the event. Generally, we get rave reviews, but we are still making slight modifications to the format. Last year we did passed tapas and, based on input, switched to a sit-down meal this year," says Peggy O'Lea, executive director of the foundation.

A lot of thought goes into deciding which culture to feature each year. "We decided on Spain the first year because a board member had recently visited there, and we felt it would be a fun country. "Our objective was to focus on countries with very diverse cultures," says O'Lea. "The second year, we initially chose Japan (before the earthquake) but changed to Germany, because we were concerned the public would think this was a fundraiser for Japanese relief efforts. We thought about Tahiti but were not excited about the décor and menu options. We also thought about Italy and Greece but didn't want to compete with existing efforts in our community so ultimately decided on Germany. Although it was still a European country, we felt the décor and cuisine would be very different," she says. Plans are already in the works for next year's event, which will feature Brazil. "We wanted a different continent and felt Brazil would be a good choice because of the publicity regarding the Olympics," she adds.

When planning a culture-themed event, O'Lea says it's important to find the right location that can meet all your needs. "For the first year, the challenge was the venue. We used the Shasta Senior Nutrition Center, because we felt the building complemented our Spanish décor. However, we had to do much of the preparation work, because a lot is not provided by the facility. With the change to the Holiday Inn for Taste of Germany, preparation was much easier," she says.

The Taste of Germany netted more than $41,000. The Foundation budgeted $30,000 for event expenses but was able to keep the costs below that number. Both years nearly 200 people attended the event. Tickets cost $75 per person or table sponsorships for eight people were available for $1,000 to $5,000.

Planning takes a core committee of about 10 people who meet monthly during most of the year. The board of directors of the foundation is in charge of finding sponsors and auction items. The day of the event 12 to 15 volunteers are recruited to help people check in/check out and monitor the silent auction. Organizers also use a computer software program called Auction Tracker to help track attendance and auction items.

Source: Peggy O'Lea, Executive Director, Shasta Library Foundation, Redding, CA.
E-mail: info@shastalibraryfoundation.org

Recruit Local Bank To Help Collect Payments

When it comes to collecting money on the day of a large fundraiser, Peggy O'Lea, executive director for the Shasta Library Foundation (Redding, CA) recommends teaming up with a local bank. O'Lea helped organize the Foundation's Taste of Germany fundraiser which raised nearly $41,000. "We get great assistance from Redding Bank of Commerce with collecting payments and processing credit cards," she says.

Fundraising for Libraries: How to Plan Profitable Special Events

Target Those You Want Your Events to Reach

Veteran event planners will often plan a series of special events to take place throughout the year. Doing so helps everyone involved do a much better job of planning.

One reason for planning a year of events in advance is that it allows you to target whom you want to attend each anticipated event.

Some events are high-end and geared to attract persons with higher discretionary income. The goal of other events might be to generate high numbers of attendees at a lower price. Still others may be targeted to particular age groups.

Ask yourself in advance what you want each special event to accomplish.

Is the primary goal to raise money? Is it to increase pub-lic awareness of your library and its programs and services? The goal of each event will help to determine whom you should target.

By putting advance thought into whom you want to attract, you can reach out to different audiences throughout the year and broaden your base of support and visibility.

The following examples of demographic criteria will help you evaluate exactly whom you want to reach:

- ✓ Careers
- ✓ Gender
- ✓ Age
- ✓ Families, singles
- ✓ Avocations
- ✓ Place of residence
- ✓ Different nationalities or ethnicities

Five Steps to Engage the Wealthy in Your Event

Every library enjoys having a base of wealthy supporters, but too often these important persons make generous contributions without attending fundraising events.

Take steps to change that, realizing that the presence of these key supporters at your special events helps to publicly convey the message that your mission is important and worth others' support.

Employ these strategies to attract persons of wealth — and their friends — to your next gala.

1. **Ask them to host a table.** As most people do, many wealthy people enjoy a bargain or having someone else occasionally offer to pick up the tab. Give these key players two complimentary tickets for hosting a group of eight to 10 attendees who pay full price.
2. **Recognize their contributions.** Awards of appreciation for support can help ensure that not only the individual, but also his or her friends and family will attend the event to be present for the recognition.

3. **Tell them their presence is crucial and meaningful.** Be direct. Tell the persons whom you most want to attend your function that they do indeed make a difference because of their standing and respect in the community. Note specific examples for each person, explaining that potential supporters who admire the individuals and their actions may be moved to become active in your library.
4. **Play down the glitz factor.** While your event may be the community's over-the-top gala of the year, that may also be the reason some very wealthy people send money but skip the party. Encourage them to attend to meet newcomers who have become involved since they last attended a major function, and to see old friends.
5. **Target them for specific events.** Does the folksy but reclusive millionaire who sends quarterly contributions fit in best at a black-tie dinner or a down-home barbecue? Instead of hoping he will simply show up at both, personally ask him to come to the event that will be the most fun. Ask for his suggestions for entertainment.

Focus on Trends to Attract Generation Y Members

Attracting younger audiences to your special events requires some understanding of causes that are important to Generation Y and some of the challenges they face in today's economic and social climate. To draw this group of people to your next special event:

- ✓ **Keep your event casual and affordable.** While younger supporters may be prosperous, formal attire at gala dinners is more attractive to their parents. Consider a tapas buffet and menu of creative cocktails or beverages. The event should include some of the same elements that they might choose on a night out with friends.
- ✓ **Think globally, act locally.** The environment, climate change and human rights are some of Generation Y's

significant issues. Emphasize ways your event will benefit at least one of those issues.

- ✓ **Have a positive focus on the future.** Generation Y has grown up with a constant drumbeat of negative news about the world from cable TV and the Internet. Make your fundraiser about the great strides your library is making in improving educational opportunities for underserved groups.
- ✓ **Tailor your event to a specific group.** The older Generation Y tier may have young children, while the later ones may not yet be able to consume alcohol. Some may be CEOs, some working in fast-food jobs. Think of trends that appeal to both and build your event around them.

Fundraising for Libraries: How to Plan Profitable Special Events

Pre-event Planning: First Steps

Develop a well thought-out special event plan, then put it in writing. Your plan should answer some key questions: What's the mission of the event; what do we want it to accomplish? Who's the target audience? How much do we expect to generate in revenue? How much will the event net? Where should it be held? Who and how many volunteers should be involved? How will we promote the event? What sort of timeline will this event include?

Seven Steps for Building a More Successful Fundraiser

Good fundraising events take far more time and effort than most people expect, says James Reber, a San Jose, CA-based consultant and author of the upcoming book, "Creating a Signature Event."

Reber offers practical advice for making any fundraiser more sustainable, effective and profitable.

1. **Understand the mission of the event.** Many libraries believe the point of a fundraiser is to generate a targeted amount of revenue, but Reber says that view is overly simplistic. "Whenever you hold an event, you a have captive audience, and if you don't educate them, motivate them and deliver key messages to them, you may have gotten money in the short term, but won't have support in the long term," he says. "Just making money that night is not enough."

2. **Select an appropriate venue.** A venue should be comfortable, convenient and should further the narrative of the event by both accentuating a library's positives and minimizing its negatives, says Reber. For example, he once advised an organization that had concerns about the turnout it would achieve to hold its event in a theater instead of a hotel. "The darkness and split-level seating masked how many people came (or didn't come), making the event feel like a success, regardless of the final attendance," he says.

3. **Draft a written event plan.** Reber says putting a plan in writing improves thinking because, "You can't gloss over details when it's in black and white in front of you." He says an event plan should be at least eight to nine pages and should include the mission/purpose of the event, its goals, measurable objectives and organizational structure. It should also have pages for discreet areas of planning such as marketing, ticket sales, venue selection and budgeting.

4. **Manage the flow of the event.** A fundraiser is a scripted event that should have a clear beginning, middle and end, says Reber. The sequence of events should convey a clear sense of direction and organizers should actively lead the audience through the event. Things that Reber says break the flow of an event include scheduling overly long programs, thanking numerous people at the start of an event — thank them at the end, when the audience

has more context of who they are, he suggests — and expecting the audience's full attention with distractions like dessert being served or auction items being opened for display.

5. **Create an emotional moment.** An emotional moment is an instant that makes the audience aware of the human importance of a library's work, and every event needs one, says Reber. He says all emotional moments are fundamentally the same: "It's a story of transformation, a human being saying, 'I was this until I met this organization, and now I'm that.'" Whether it is the troubled youth who just earned his diploma, the illiterate mother who now heads the library's literacy program or any other example, transformation is key to an emotionally powerful event.

6. **Highlight the messages to be taken from the event.** Every event should have two or three messages audience members will be able to articulate after they leave, says Reber. "Maybe the messages are that we're growing, we're providing services to more people than ever, and your dollars are making it all possible." Whatever the circumstances, Reber says central themes should be reflected throughout the event, from the introduction, keynote address and emotional moment to the printed program, centerpieces and décor.

7. **Plan to repeat and expand the event.** Never plan an event that cannot be repeated and expanded, says Reber. Expansion can be internal — prices to a sold-out event can be raised, for example — but current-year plans should always have an eye toward long-term growth.

Source: James Reber, Consultant and Author, San Jose, CA.
E-mail: james@jamesreber.com

Special Events Tip

- After booking the location for a special event, find out who will be using that space ahead of you. They may have certain materials — decorations, lighting, equipment and more — that would work in nicely with your event.

Fundraising for Libraries: How to Plan Profitable Special Events

Key Questions to Ask Before Taking on a New Event

If you're thinking about boosting your library's fundraising plan with a new event, make sure you ask the right questions to guarantee that it's worth your time and energy. Here are some things to consider:

1. Is there a less labor-intensive way to raise the same amount of money?

2. How saturated is your market with charitable events? What kind of event is missing? How can your library help fill that gap? What kind of audience is not being targeted?

3. Who will be responsible for planning the event (staff, volunteers, etc.)? How will this impact their other duties?

4. What is the real cost of the event — not just in expenses, but also in staff and volunteer time?

5. What is a realistic amount you can charge for entrance in your market? Is that enough, once expenditures are taken out, to make the event worthwhile?

6. What will make your event stand out from other charitable events in the area?

7. How can you keep expenses down?

8. Is the event you're considering a good match for your constituents?

9. Do you have a mailing list that will support the kind of event you're considering? If not, how will you market the event to attract supporters?

10. How will you evaluate the success of the event?

Library Event Profile

Sew Wut Goes Into Planning a Spelling Bee?

If you ask Donna Hylton how to spell fundraiser, she'll respond, "S-P-E-L-L-I-N-G B-E-E."

Hylton is the executive director of the Kern Adult Literacy Council (Bakersfield, CA) which has been successfully raising thousands of dollars for the past 22 years by simply asking people to spell. "It's not our largest fundraiser, but it's the easiest to organize. Plus — best of all — there are no expenses that go into planning a spelling bee! Once you have a location, all you need are two microphones and some sort of buzzer. We use a cow bell," says Hylton. Hylton gets the words online from the Scripps National Spelling Bee official word list and she e-mails all participants that list about a week before the bee so they have some time to study.

But what makes the Kern ALC Spelling Bee unique is the amount of money that is raised. "We raise anywhere from $5,000 to $12,000 each year. I have people ask me how I can raise that much money at a spelling bee, and I tell them when looking for participants, approach companies and service organizations and charge a high entry fee," she says.

The Kern ALC Spelling Bee has three entry fee levels: $500, $1,000 and $1,500; and the more a team pays, the more additional chances they get to stay in the game.

Occasionally Hylton will come across a business or organization that would like to sponsor a team, but no one from that company wants to participate. In those cases Hylton plays the role of matchmaker. "I've had people come up to me and say they'd love to participate, but they can't afford it, so I team them up with a company willing to pay," she says.

When asked what the most challenging part of planning an adult spelling bee is, Hylton says in the first few years recruiting teams of two can be a struggle. "Now a days not many people spell well and people are reluctant to get up in front of an audience. But once they do it, they have so much fun and want to come back year after year," she says.

The winning team is given a donated plaque as well as a Barnes & Noble gift card. Hylton recruits local celebrities to act as judges and uses a professor from an area college to be the pronouncer. "It's very important to have someone who can pronounce all the words clearly and correctly," she says.

Typically more than 100 people show up to watch the spelling bee, which takes place on a Thursday night from 7:00 to 9:00 at a Bakersfield Barnes & Noble bookstore. Teaming up with Barnes & Noble also has its benefits. "The day of the spelling bee, the store donates a portion of its sales to the Kern Adult Literacy Council. I hand out flyers to those who attend to encourage them to buy a book that day to help our cause. It's a great added bonus," she says.

Source: Donna Hylton, Executive Director, Kern Adult Literacy Council, Bakersfield, CA. E-mail: dohylto@zeus.kern.org

Use Checklists to Make Events More Manageable

Special event planning can seem overwhelming. With the date growing steadily nearer and the to-do list growing longer, how will you ever get everything accomplished by the big day?

Don't become paralyzed by the feeling of not knowing where to begin. Rather, put pen to paper today and develop a checklist that you can either share with others or use yourself to track and monitor event planning progress. Doing so will make the tasks and many deadlines seem much more manageable.

Here's how to create an effective checklist for your next event:

1. **Start making a list.** Begin by thinking about and listing everything you can imagine that will need to be done, regardless of who is responsible for doing it. List both big-picture items and details — whatever comes to mind. Don't get caught up in prioritizing items or worrying about the order of things at this point. Carry your checklist around and keep adding items as they come to mind.

2. **Review your list and assign individual checklist items to appropriate categories.** As you develop a list of everything you can imagine that will need to happen at some point along the way, the entire event — from start to finish — will become more clear in your mind. You can now begin to group individual actions into common categories (e.g., invitations and ticket sales, sponsorships, hospitality, program, location and so on). The completion of these groupings helps to provide a big-picture view of the project and points out gaps among actions that will need to occur. Fill these gaps with additional needed checklist items.

3. **Assign deadlines and persons responsible for each checklist item.** Once your checklist is relatively complete add details as you think of them, organize your list by category and chronology. Assign a deadline date to each checklist item along with names of persons responsible for completion. This process will help you transform your checklist into a timetable as well.

The creation of an event checklist will help you better visualize what needs to take place from start to finish and also helps to keep you and others on track. Use this example to get started on yours:

Checklist for May 23, 2013 Special Event

Action Item	Responsible Persons	Deadline	Action Item	Responsible Persons	Deadline
PRE-EVENT			**DURING EVENT**		
☐ Select program speaker	Gard	10/10/12	☐ Take tickets	Marcus	5/23
☐ Enlist project committee	Gard	1/3/13	☐ Handle general and special seating	Holt	5/23
☐ Schedule regular committee meetings	Gard	1/8	☐ Oversee meal	Holt	5/23
☐ Cmte. members recruit sub-committee members	Holt/Wen	1/22	☐ Oversee music and sound system	Holt	5/23
☐ Planning meeting	Gard	1/23	☐ Host speaker	Gard	5/23
☐ Decide on location	Holt	2/4	☐ Seat head table	Gard	5/23
☐ Order sound system	Holt	2/4	☐ Event publicity	Wen	5/23
☐ Design invitations	Wen	3/14			
☐ Sell tickets — individual or tables of 10	Marcus	4/14	**POST EVENT**		
☐ Place advertising	Wen	5/6	☐ Speaker to airport	Gard	5/23
☐ Design & print program	Wen	5/6	☐ Clean-up crew	Holt	5/23
☐ Send invitations	Wen	5/6	☐ Follow-up correspondence	Gard	5/27
☐ Arrange for head table	Gard	5/7	☐ Evaluate event	Gard	6/11
☐ Conduct publicity for the effort	Wen	5/10	☐ Pick date for next year	All	6/11
☐ Decorate facility	Holt	5/22			

Fundraising for Libraries: How to Plan Profitable Special Events

Become Familiar With Your Community's Events

If you'd like to plan a new special event, it would be worth the time to first examine your community's existing events:

- What time of year are they held and by what organizations?
- How many people attend, and what is the makeup of attendees?

Knowing answers to these questions will help you determine the best event for you.

Map Each Step of First-time Events — Backwards

If you library board is planning a new special event, the best method for determining what needs to be done along the way is to pinpoint a date and then work backwards.

Once you determine the type of event and the date, you can think through each step. By working backwards, you can better visualize important details — everything from identifying the perfect location to sending invitations to hanging decorations and more.

As you keep coming up with your timeline of tasks and corresponding dates, be sure to list beside each task the name of the individual who is responsible for completing the task.

Use Checklist to Guide You Through Planning a Gala

If your main event is a gala, you know how crucial it is to be organized and prepared. To help you plan and maximize your event success, start with a simple initial planning checklist, using this example to create one that fits your library's specific needs:

Gala Planning Checklist

Name of Event: _____
Date: _____
Time: _____
Location: _____
Event Purpose: _____

INITIAL PLANNING STAGES
- ☐ How many guests are expected?_____
- ☐ How many volunteers are needed to plan a seamless event? _____
- ☐ Do we have the resources to make it happen?_____
- ☐ Coordinate planning committee and assign officers to each stage below.

SCHEDULING
Officer in charge: _____
Planning Committee Members: _____
_____

- ☐ Determine the size of the event space needed.
- ☐ Determine the type of technical needs the event will require.
- ☐ Tentatively book two possible dates for the event.
- ☐ Contact necessary vendors to schedule the event date.
- ☐ Call the reservation office to confirm your event date.
- ☐ Schedule a meeting to review event seating and guest needs.

PERMITS
Officer in charge: _____
- ☐ Food Permit
- ☐ Alcohol Permit
- ☐ Sanitation Permit
- ☐ Security Scheduled
- ☐ Outdoor Space Permit
- ☐ Sound Permit
- ☐ Fundraising Permit

ADVERTISING
Officer in charge: _____
- ☐ Poster placement
- ☐ E-mail LISTSERVs or e-mail blasts
- ☐ Media advertising placement: print, Web, television, radio

Event Preplanning Involves Determining Event Details

When preplanning a new event, it's important to secure valuable information before bringing others into the planning stages.

Use the following preplanning guide to assist as you speak to staff, volunteers and vendors about your newest event:

- ☐ Date of event
- ☐ Purpose of event
- ☐ Event start and end time
- ☐ Number of people expected to attend
- ☐ Venue preference
- ☐ Event title
- ☐ Potential sponsors/donors
- ☐ Event type (meeting, banquet, special event, etc.)
- ☐ Target audience
- ☐ Special equipment needs
- ☐ Preliminary budget
- ☐ Food/refreshment needs
- ☐ Program/entertainment

Use Creativity When Designing Event Invitations

Invitations to your library's events need not be costly to be effective or memorable. Let these ideas get you started and inspire your creative team:

❑ **Try business card invitations.** The who, what, when, where and why of most events can fit on a blank printable business card, especially if the event is open to the public and formal mailing lists aren't needed. Leave stacks at businesses, distribute at networking events and have volunteers hand them out.

❑ **Carefully evaluate needs.** Will your invitation design have equal impact with just one or two colors? A well-executed graphic and attractive layout can look great in black or grayscale and cost less than more colorful versions.

❑ **Stick it!** Shop the marketplace for bright adhesive stickers in interesting shapes and design your basic invitation to accommodate them in the design theme. Besides using them on the invitation, add them to the mailing envelope and response cards.

❑ **Use surplus materials in your inventory.** Take a tip from Scarlett O'Hara, who made a gown from drapes. Leftover blank envelopes and outdated letterhead trimmed to size can be a blank canvas for your invitation.

❑ **Consider using plantable, printable paper.** Seeded papers, party favors, place cards and even confetti are available from online retailers and specialty stores. When planted, they grow into flowers.

❑ **Look online for ready-made cards.** Sourcing artwork and design on invitation websites helps you obtain professional-looking results and saves money and time. Dozens of online retailers offer broad selections of stock images with themes for total invitation packages that are printed and shipped within a week or two. Some also will provide matching artwork for e-cards.

❑ **Vary materials.** Consider integrating into your invitation design a swatch of colorful fabric, unique twine, die-cut flower or other shape, spiced tea bag or other small items that fit your event theme. They can add color, interest and context when appropriately used.

Use E-Invitations to Save Costs, Expedite Your Message

One of the simplest and most cost-effective ways to save on your event planning budget is to eliminate paper invitations and replace them with e-invitations. E-invitations require no mailing labels, stamps or envelopes.

E-invitations can replace an event invitation or can be used to complement one. If your next event still requires the mailing of an invitation, use an e-invitation as a follow-up reminder to the hard copy that was mailed. Doing so will ensure guests will still receive an invitation even if the hard copy gets lost in the mail.

Here are five websites that offer free e-invitations:

- www.evite.com
- www.sendomatic.com
- www.smilebox.com
- www.invite-o-matic.com
- www.mypunchbowl.com

Popular Event? Send Invitations in Phases

If you're fortunate enough to have an annual event that has grown so popular you're forced to limit attendance, consider sending invitations in phases. Here's how:

1. First decide who should get top priority — those who have attended in the past? Board members? Your largest donors? Would-be donors?

2. Next, prioritize your guest list, separating invitees into two or more groups. Send the first batch of invitations with an RSVP deadline far enough in advance of your event to tally replies and know how many of the second (or more) group of invitations to send. (That number will be determined by the response you get from the first group.)

3. While you might expect a small percentage of cancellations, be cautious about over-booking, so you have a handful of seats for last-minute additions you wish to make.

"A library is not a luxury but one of the necessities of life."

— *Henry Ward Beecher*

Fundraising for Libraries: How to Plan Profitable Special Events.
Edited by Scott C. Stevenson.
© 2012 Stevenson, Inc. Published 2012 by Stevenson, Inc.

Fundraising for Libraries: How to Plan Profitable Special Events

Creating a Budget to Visualize Profit

If a key goal of your special event is to make money for your library, then the budget becomes the centerpiece of your planning efforts. Not only is it important to anticipate what it will take to make a worthwhile profit, it's also important for everyone involved to know how to keep a lid on expenses. Every idea, whether you're planning a gala, a mystery dinner, a spelling bee or a lecture, should be backed with a plan for how to pay for it.

Create First-time Event Budget

With so many factors to consider — from food to entertainment to decorations — how do you build a budget for a first-time event?

"The key is understanding costs for individual segments of the budget," says Cathy Genetti, president and founder of Next Level Event Design (Chicago, IL). "You need to know what to expect and what to budget for." Also, she says, have a not-to-exceed budget number as early in the planning process as possible.

Genetti shares steps she takes to help a nonprofit client determine a budget for a first-time fundraiser:

1. **Get a clear understanding of the library's demographic**, events it has offered, the outcome of those events, and if they met expectations.

2. **Know the event goal.** The primary goal shouldn't be to raise money, but could be to create a closer community or increase awareness. Is there a call to action for the guests? What should be the emotional take-away?

3. **Articulate expectations and a shared definition of success.** Be realistic when planning an inaugural event and creating a count goal.

4. **Research other events in your area** that may impact attendance.

5. **Determine how much money the event is expected to raise**, then do the math. Are sponsors or sponsorship opportunities involved? What is an appropriate ticket price for this demographic? Will ticket price merely cover the cost of the per-person price? How will additional sums be raised?

6. **Estimate the hours needed to produce the event**, including meetings, conference calls, walk-throughs and production time. Over-estimate to accommodate unknown issues.

7. **Check with stakeholders** to make sure the initial rough figure will work for them.

"Normally there's one aspect of an event that is a main focus — it could be entertainment, food, lighting and décor, etc.," Genetti says. "Once you know this, you can earmark how much money you can allot to each category, so that you can give this information to your vendors."

Source: Cathy Genetti, President and Founder, Next Level Event Design, Chicago, IL. E-mail: www.NextLevelEventDesign.com

Watching the Pennies: Creating an Event Budget

When creating a budget for your next event, follow this checklist for properly accounting for and tracking expenses:

❑ Work closely with your caterer to determine food and beverage costs. Don't forget to build in the cost of gratuity for the wait staff, which can be up to 20 percent above and beyond the caterer's total.

❑ If your event will require equipment rental, note all fees and build a cushion for cost of breakage and late fees.

❑ Itemize cost of gifts for guests, staff and/or volunteers. No matter how economical the gift, costs can add up due to number of items purchased.

❑ Calculate cost of transportation to include shuttles that may be provided to guests, as well as driver tips.

❑ When choosing the event site, obtain a bid from at least three potential sites to determine the best value. Build in extra for costs associated with early set up and tear down of the event.

❑ If you're holding your event outdoors, account for tent, table, chair and toileting facility rental.

❑ Allow for a contingency fund. Estimate approximately 10 to 20 percent of your total to a slush fund that allows for extras that were overlooked.

❑ Summarize your costs and review them again. Look meticulously for areas in which you can pare back to save expense without compromising guest comfort or the quality of your event.

> ### Event Budgeting Tip
>
> ■ When exploring the possibility of a first-time fundraising event, here's one way to project net proceeds: Plan to cover all costs of your event with sponsor support. That way, all other revenue generated will be pure profit.

Event Planning Worksheet Helps Anticipate Revenue, Expenses

How do you know if a new or altered fundraising event will generate enough revenue to cover expenses and still make a profit?

Make use of a budget worksheet to map first-time events. The worksheet helps organizers view the entire scope of a project, including all the hidden costs, before committing manpower and resources to it.

Past events have a history, and organizers merely need to refer to the prior year's budget and records for guidance. But entirely new undertakings are a different matter. Complete the worksheet below for every first-time event, then take time to evaluate the numbers. The worksheet can be used to ensures that everyone involved is on the same page and working toward the same goals.

Complete a worksheet such as the example shown here at least three months into the event planning. A worksheet helps everyone recognize the expenses up front, including all the incidentals (flowers, table decorations, etc.) that add up quickly.

The first section of the worksheet identifies revenue-generating goals like sponsorships, individual donations, auction proceeds and ticket sales. The next section identifies expenses. The final section shows how revenue, minus expenses, equals an anticipated financial gain.

If revenues are in line with expenses, the event can be given the go-ahead. If not, organizers can revamp their goals by raising ticket prices, recruiting more sponsors, adding more auction items or deciding how expenses might be reduced.

Content not available in this edition

Library Event Profile

Novel Night Proves to Be Novel Fundraiser

Event planners couldn't have asked for a better ending to the inaugural Novel Night to benefit the Hoboken Public Library (Hoboken, NJ).

While they had hoped for eight dinner hosts and 100 guests, they ended up with 16 hosts and more than 150 guests, raising nearly $22,000.

Ruth Charnes, former president of Friends of Hoboken Library, explains how the event, which marked its second year in October 2008, worked:

Volunteers open their homes to between eight and 20 guests for book-themed dinners. The meal idea and expense is the host's tax-deductible donation. Information is posted on the Internet and invitations are sent by e-mail and regular mail.

Guests pay $100 to attend and rank their top five dinner/book choices when they reply. They learn which dinner party they will attend a week before the event. Charnes says most people are matched with one of their top five choices.

Dinner parties begin at 7:30 p.m. at individual homes, then conclude with dessert being served at 10 p.m. at a common location. For 2008, the event concluded at the library, providing a great opportunity to show it off.

Charnes says the creativity and generosity of the hosts are keys to the event's success.

"We have people who are willing to open their homes at considerable effort and expense," she says. "There was such energy and excitement at the end of the evening last year. People were saying, 'Let me tell you about my dinner.' Guests had such a great time, the only complaint we got was that the time was too short."

Contributing to the event's success, she notes, is the community's small size. "People are easily able to walk to each other's homes and then walk to the library for dessert. We didn't have to worry about parking or driving 40 miles to get to your host's home."

The event raises funds for the preservation of the library's historic materials.

Source: Ruth Charnes, former President, Friends of Hoboken Library, Hoboken, NJ. E-mail: novelnight@gmail.com

Content not available in this edition

Books Inspire Hosts, Dinner Themes

Ruth Charnes, president, Friends of Hoboken Public Library (Hoboken, NJ), shares examples of dinners served at the inaugural Novel Night in 2007:

The concept of books coming to life is apparent in this invitation to an evening of book-themed meals at volunteers' homes, which raises money for the Hoboken Public Library (Hoboken, NJ):

- **"A Tale of Two Cities" by Charles Dickens.** The hosts, whose apartment offered a spectacular view of New York City, featured foods typical of New York and Hoboken.

- **"Pedrito's World" by Arturo Martinez.** This dinner, hosted by the author himself, featured food and drinks from his Southwestern childhood including tamales, enchiladas, margaritas and Mexican hot chocolate.

- **"Team of Rivals" by Doris Kearns Goodwin.** Within a beautifully restored Victorian mansion, hosts dressed in Victorian costumes and served a menu of foods from the North and South including stewed oysters, catfish and venison.

- **"Zohra's Ladder and Other Moroccan Tales" by Pamela Windo.** Hosts created an indoor tent and served a Moroccan menu with various salads, spinach "cigars" and couscous. Guests had the chance to meet the author, who was in attendance, and made and served Moroccan sweet mint tea.

Eight Budget-saving Tips

To save money on your next event, consider each of these eight cost-cutting measures:

1. Go with food stations rather than a plated meal.

2. If you're planning to serve alcohol at your event, consider having beer and wine and a signature drink instead of an open bar.

3. Rather than pay someone to design your invitation or other materials, turn it into a contest. Provide a detailed spec sheet of what you have in mind, and offer a prize to the winning designer.

4. Select a venue that won't require the level of decoration that say, a hotel room would require (e.g., art gallery, corporate lobby, garden).

5. Weigh the possibility of having a mid-morning or afternoon event that won't involve a full meal and numerous drinks per person.

6. Consider a Sunday afternoon rather than a Saturday night. Many vendors will work with you on price if you are not booking them for their prime time.

7. When it comes to printing needs, ask printers to compare your choices of paper or cardstock with any overstock they may have on hand.

8. Rather than a full seated dinner, create appetizer and small plate menus that will be equally well-received but cost less.

Budget Estimate Helps in Planning Stages

Before jumping into any new library event, take the time to formulate a budget estimate complete with projected costs and revenue.

You need not be exact in projecting an event's expenses and revenue, but the very process of thinking through each component of your event will begin to give you some idea of what may need to be done to project net income, increase revenue or decrease expenses. You may even decide that a particular event can't be justified based on the estimated budget.

The budget planning process will force you to make decisions about issues such as: program, entertainment, food/refreshments, venue, sources of revenue and more. That procedure will help you arrive at decisions that you may not fully consider in the absence of an event budget estimate.

Use the form shown here as a template to create your own event budget estimate. Share it with others on your staff or those helping with your event to get their input on anticipated costs and revenue.

Content not available in this edition

Fundraising for Libraries: How to Plan Profitable Special Events.
Edited by Scott C. Stevenson.
© 2012 Stevenson, Inc. Published 2012 by Stevenson, Inc.

Fundraising for Libraries: How to Plan Profitable Special Events

Outlining an Organizational Structure

Your event's organizational structure will be shaped by your friends of the library leadership, the number of volunteers required to implement and carry out the event, the types of committees required and the tasks needed to be carried out prior to and during the event. Some events can get by with only a handful of volunteers, while others require hundreds of committed helpers. Some events have a variety of committee types, and others rely on only two or three committees to get the job done.

Event Characteristics Determine Volunteer Needs

Before scrambling to find capable volunteers, it makes sense to identify the unique characteristics of each anticipated event planned by your library. Doing so will help identify the types of volunteers needed as well as required numbers of volunteers, skills needed, anticipated work hours and more.

Content not available in this edition

The benefits of identifying each event's characteristics in advance are twofold: 1) The event will be completed more thoroughly and successfully with the right volunteer match, and 2) those involved with the event will find the experience more accommodating and rewarding.

A form similar to the one at left can be used by your office as well as other offices requiring the services of volunteers. Make the forms available to interested staff throughout your library, and ask that all event forms be completed and returned to you far in advance of event planning to provide adequate matching, recruiting and training time.

Enlist an Event Intern's Help

Could you use some extra help planning your events? Recruit a college intern to help with certain aspects of your work.

Students majoring in public relations, marketing, business or related fields may relish the opportunity to get some hands-on experience with event planning.

Begin by identifying specific and meaningful tasks that could be completed by an intern. Avoid busy work or mundane assignments. A special event intern's tasks might include:
- Working to publicize an event.
- Designing an event logo and poster.
- Serving as your liaison during committee meetings.
- Helping manage details at the event.
- Helping evaluate a completed event.
- Assisting with sponsorship efforts.
- Helping recruit and manage volunteers.

With a list of proposed intern tasks in hand, create a job description that outlines responsibilities to be performed throughout the duration of the internship.

Whether the internship lasts a month or a semester, you can provide great educational opportunities for interns while getting extra help planning your event.

Library Event Profile

Library Volunteers Celebrate 20 Years of Success

Officials with the Friends of the Waccamaw Library (Pawleys Island, SC) could write a book about how to hold a successful book sale.

For two decades, the organization — created to raise awareness and use of the Waccamaw Neck Branch Library (Georgetown, SC) — has generated increasingly profitable sales, with proceeds funding the library's children's program and the children's librarian position.

Roslind Briet, chairperson for the 2010 book sale, held July 8-10, says that when the annual event began two decades ago, it involved only a few shelves in the back of the library.

"The sale grew and was moved into the library conference room," Briet says. "It grew a third time and is now held in the Family Life Center of the St. Paul's Waccamaw United Methodist Church."

The July 2010 event netted nearly $12,000 and attracted some 500 attendees.

Briet credits volunteers for the sale's success. Throughout the year, she says, volunteers collect and sort donated books and other items. For the sale, they set up, keep tables filled with books, collect the money, make signs, distribute fliers, and make sure the books and other items — all of which are donated — are in mint condition. They even pick up donations if persons are unable to get to the library.

But perhaps the two most important elements of a profitable sale have to do with the quality of the donated items and how those items are organized.

Briet says planning for the event and organizing the books takes a full year and is an ongoing process. Books are arranged in 50 broad categories and alphabetized by author. Signs displayed over the books identify categories, so buyers can venture directly to their area of interest.

"The secret is in the set-up," she says. "Our patrons appreciate the fact that the books are not just out on a table for them to hunt through, but are organized into categories."

In fact, the sale has been so popular, Briet says shoppers come from all over the country, with some timing their vacation to coincide with the sale.

Other supporters have found other ways to become involved, she says. "This year, a resident who was a retired New York City musician donated his LP record collection dating from the 1930s (and) our patrons found some real gems for 25 cents. The fun people have sharing their finds with friends and family makes all the hard work worthwhile."

Source: Roslind Briet, Chairperson, Annual Book Sale, Friends of the Waccamaw Library, Pawleys Island, SC.

At a Glance —	
Event Type:	Annual Book Sale
Gross:	$12,600
Costs:	$800
Net Income:	$11,800
Volunteers:	60
Planning:	Year-round
Attendees:	500
Revenue Sources:	Sales of donated books
Unique Feature:	Volunteers sort books by category and author to simplify shopping

Ease Would-be Volunteers Into Your Events

Involving people in the life and work of an organization is the best way for them to begin to own and become committed to it.

All too often, however, we turn would-be volunteers away by forcing too much on them too fast. This is especially true for event volunteers, who can easily feel overwhelmed by too much, too soon, and end up walking away.

To establish a long-term volunteer relationship, be sensitive to the circumstances of those you are trying to recruit, spoon-feeding opportunities for involvement.

Rather than inviting a newcomer to take on too much too fast, try these methods:

✓ **Learn what interests them.** Rather than saying, "We could sure use your help taking tickets for our eight-hour event," get to know what makes the person tick. What are his/her likes and dislikes? How much time might he/she have available?

✓ **Expose them to snapshots of your organization's work.** Don't overwhelm individuals by sharing more than they want to know. Instead, share glimpses of your library and its special events over time, so they can grow familiar with it gradually.

✓ **Share entry-level involvement opportunties.** Share subtle involvement options from time to time: "This committee has about five regular volunteers, but they could use more help." Make it obvious that all levels of involvement are available. Create and share an event planning list with various volunteer opportunities based on amount of time/effort required.

✓ **Help them feel comfortable.** Eliminate anxiety by introducing would-be volunteers to others associated with your event, making it clear they need only take on projects they choose.

How to Ask Someone to Lead Your Special Event

Do you have someone in mind to chair your next big event?

Once you have decided whom you want to head up your library's event, it's important to approach him/her in a way that will support its eventual success.

Use the following guidelines when enlisting a key volunteer:

❑ **Meet face to face.** Don't attempt to enlist a leader by phone or e-mail. Doing so will diminish the event's importance while making it difficult to convey the entirety of what will be expected. Use phone or e-mail to set up a face-to-face meeting time where you make your pitch.

❑ **Be honest about why this person is the right person.** Tell the individual why it's important to have him/her lead the event. The person will be more likely to assume the role with greater enthusiasm, if he/she feels able to make a noticeable difference.

❑ **Explain the project thoroughly.** Walk through each step of the event, explaining what needs to happen along the way, and your leadership prospect's role in that process. Include a written explanation of the person's role at each phase. Be as complete as possible, so you both visualize the same process from start to finish.

❑ **Go over the ways in which the individual will be supported.** What will staff's role be throughout the process? Who will be the leader's internal contact? How much of the leadership role involves actual decision making and how much is for appearance sake? What happens if things go wrong?

❑ **Give the individual time to consider your request.** Leave a written outline of the event with the individual asking him/her to give it some thought before making a decision. Agree on a mutually acceptable time frame for the consideration process, then meet once again to answer any questions and hear the person's decision.

This deliberate approach to selecting a leader will make for a more enthused and committed individual in the end.

Have Event Backup Plan In Case Chair Drops Out

The success of any important charitable event depends upon an effective chairperson and a team of experienced volunteers — not the chairperson alone. If for any reason the chairperson of your event suddenly departs, a backup plan including the following strategies will keep the effort moving forward with minimal disruption:

✓ **Prepare your vice chair.** This person will attend all major planning sessions, ideally with the plan that he or she will serve as chair the following year.

✓ **Ask past chairs to be advisors.** If they are willing, a team of past chairs who will serve as resources to current chairs and vice chairs can rally to assist the person who must assume the former-chairperson's duties.

✓ **Gather committee co-chairs.** Determine which committees are best prepared to take over various tasks, dividing the duties as equally as possible.

✓ **Be alert for signs of difficulty.** There may be advance warnings that your chair is unable or unwilling to complete all the steps necessary to ensure a successful event. Absences from meetings, lack of enthusiasm or negativity toward others' ideas can be signals that a new game plan is in order.

✓ **Remain diplomatic and nonjudgmental if your chair withdraws for nonemergency reasons.** Attempting to discuss the situation with outside parties will only derail you from the more important mission of getting plans back on track quickly.

✓ **Promote your new chair.** You may be able to parlay the change in personnel into an opportunity for extra publicity. Write press releases announcing the new chairperson, emphasizing his/her volunteer experience, dedication and enthusiasm for your event.

Quantify What You Hope to Accomplish

When planning your year's events, it makes good sense to have clearly identifiable goals with quantifiable, measurable objectives. That way, persons who are involved with planning events have a common focus, and you can judge the success of each completed event.

Here are some examples of quantifiable objectives for persons who work with and manage special events:

• To generate $X in special event net income throughout the year.

• To plan and execute X special events throughout the year.

• To attract a minimum of X cumulative attendees throughout the fiscal year based on a series of special events.

• To create a special event which targets that segment of our community capable of making major gifts.

• To keep the cost-to-revenue ratio of all events under 20 percent (e.g., $10,000 in revenue with expenses of $2,000).

• To involve no fewer than 100 volunteers in planning and carrying out special events throughout the year.

Fundraising for Libraries: How to Plan Profitable Special Events.
Edited by Scott C. Stevenson.
© 2012 Stevenson, Inc. Published 2012 by Stevenson, Inc.

Fundraising for Libraries: How to Plan Profitable Special Events

Ideas and Themes

Looking for winning themes and ideas for your library's next special event? Break the mold! Think outside the box. Here are a variety of possibilities to get your committee's neurons firing.

For Story Idea Inspiration, Turn to Your Calendar

Take a look at your calendar and you'll find a holiday or observance nearly every week and month of the year. Look for ways to connect several of those special days to your mission to generate media coverage and raise funds.

Here are some examples:

✓ **Fly your flag.** If your library supports veterans, military families or government employees like firefighters, choose holidays like Memorial Day, Flag Day or Veterans Day to give small flags to supporters, along with proper display instructions and a URL for a Web demonstration. Your local television affiliate may also be interested in getting involved.

✓ **Celebrate an artist's birthday.** If your art auction is in October, honor Pablo Picasso by holding it on or near the 25th. Salvador Dali's May 11 birthday provides limitless inspiration not only for an event, but themes and decorations. Recognizing a famous creative person gives an added spark for gaining media coverage, and there are fascinating people who were born during every month.

✓ **Travel across the globe.** Your fundraiser may already have an Asian or Latin American theme, but tying it into a real celebration somewhere in the world can give it additional meaning. You can find countless listings, dates and ideas online at websites including www.todayinhistory.com.

✓ **Observe national health and safety days.** For example, Home Safety Month is June, August is Immunization Month and December 1 is World AIDS Day. For more ideas, go to www.healthfinder.gov to match a health-related event with your cause.

✓ **Celebrate Founder's Day.** Your library or institution most likely launched on a specific day. Even if you don't have a milestone anniversary on the horizon, you can honor your founder every year on that date by creating an event or providing a community service that he or she would have supported such as stocking a food pantry, painting houses for deserving families or hosting a family picnic.

Bring On the Talent!

Whether featuring serious talent or drawing campy performers — such as your CEO playing harmonica — talent shows are almost guaranteed to attract audiences as people seek to cheer on their favorites.

But don't let too much of a good thing lessen the impact of the event by being too long, boring, or even embarrassing for entrants who are out of their elements.

Set some ground rules before soliciting participants. Here are factors to consider for your specific talent show:

❑ **Determine number and types of acts.** Hold auditions for singers, dancers, stand-up comics, instrumental musicians and more. Limit each performance to less than five minutes. Choose only the best two or three for each category to help ensure top performance quality.

❑ **Make tapes of each audition.** Put them on your website to promote the event, and to allow community votes and comments. You may need to screen to prevent spam voting and monitor remarks, but the more traffic to your show link the more public interest is generated. Use the winning clips as publicity.

❑ **Enlist celebrity judges.** Local media personalities, sports team coaches and elected officials can judge the participants and award the prizes. It also helps garner free media.

❑ **Hold at least two rehearsals.** Both informal and dress rehearsals will help you and performers work out any technical or logistical bugs in the program. You can even sell tickets to the dress rehearsal for those who cannot make the actual show.

❑ **Stagger the types of performances.** Three interpretive dancers or pianists in a row may lull the audience into complacency. Mix up the acts with singers, comics, jazz ensembles and celebrity impersonators.

❑ **Don't limit your show only to the traditional.** Someone who wants to enter your show might have a truly unusual talent, like playing guitar while suspended by his ankles on an inversion table. Unique skills that are still tasteful can be big crowd-pleasers and keep audiences guessing about what might be next.

Sponsor Competition to Name That Event

Why have a competition to name your upcoming event? Because not only can the competition result in the most creative theme, it can serve to attract people who might otherwise not become involved.

Plus, the competition adds another opportunity to generate publicity.

Here are a handful of ideas to incorporate into your event-naming competition:

1. Limit the competition to a particular group based on its potential for adding to event attendees (e.g., youth in a particular age range, members of the graduating class, persons who have been members for 10 or more years).

2. Offer a prize to the winner to motivate participation in the naming contest.

3. Appoint a panel of three to five judges from a cross-section of your library (e.g., employee, board member, volunteer) and set basic parameters for the judging.

4. Have a press conference to unveil the winning theme or name for your event. Invite the winner.

5. Consider a limited number of free event tickets or other incentive for anyone who enters the competition.

6. Introduce the winner at your event and include VIP service.

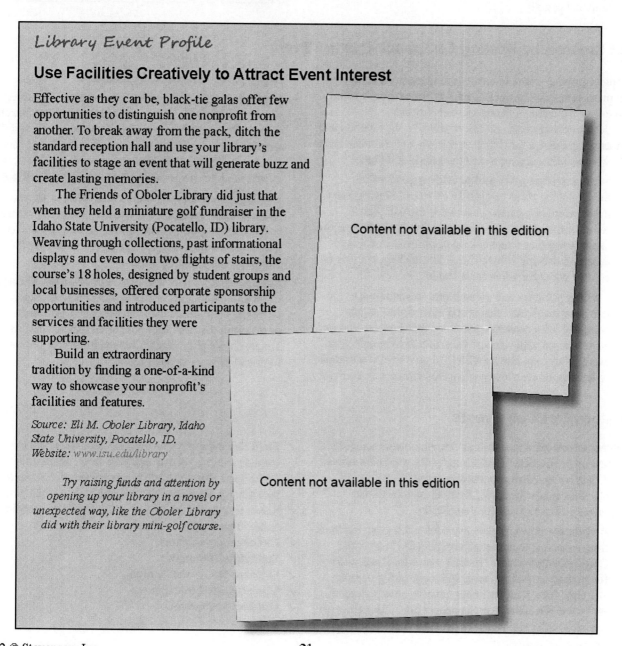

Library Event Profile

Use Facilities Creatively to Attract Event Interest

Effective as they can be, black-tie galas offer few opportunities to distinguish one nonprofit from another. To break away from the pack, ditch the standard reception hall and use your library's facilities to stage an event that will generate buzz and create lasting memories.

The Friends of Oboler Library did just that when they held a miniature golf fundraiser in the Idaho State University (Pocatello, ID) library. Weaving through collections, past informational displays and even down two flights of stairs, the course's 18 holes, designed by student groups and local businesses, offered corporate sponsorship opportunities and introduced participants to the services and facilities they were supporting.

Build an extraordinary tradition by finding a one-of-a-kind way to showcase your nonprofit's facilities and features.

Source: Eli M. Oboler Library, Idaho State University, Pocatello, ID. Website: www.isu.edu/library

Try raising funds and attention by opening up your library in a novel or unexpected way, like the Oboler Library did with their library mini-golf course.

Content not available in this edition

Content not available in this edition

Partner With Dissimilar Nonprofit for Joint Fundraiser

Looking to generate $10,000 or more in new funds? Get together with another nonprofit to organize a joint fundraising event that will benefit both organizations equally.

People love to see collaboration among nonprofit organizations, even when it's a fundraising event. Plus, both organizations involved benefit in these and other ways:

1. Introducing your nonprofit's mission to attendees who might not otherwise be familiar with or support your efforts.

2. Having at least twice the volunteer involvement in planning and coordinating the event — maybe more, if more than two nonprofits are involved — making the event less labor intensive.

3. You will have generated additional funds toward your annual fundraising goal.

Double Volunteer Numbers

Here's one more idea to maximize benefits and event proceeds by working with another volunteer-driven organization: Coordinate a one- or two-day volunteer swap for your annual special event.

Doing so is a win-win for both organizations, as long as each volunteer group owns the concept, since volunteers are the ones agreeing to give time to an organization in which they may have no particular interest. Do your part to encourage that ownership by helping them understand that helping the other group actually benefits your cause.

Get Creative by Hosting Scrapbook-themed Event

People's growing desire to create lasting memories and commemorate milestone occasions has turned scrapbooking into one of the nation's fastest-growing hobbies.

Scrapbooking events also have proved to be relaxing and lucrative fundraisers for churches, schools and charities. Here is how some of them have netted thousands of dollars:

- **Setting a ticket price and providing good value.** Scrapbooking crops can justify a $40 to $50 per person ticket price for a daylong event that includes lunch, refreshments, a flat workspace and the chance to pool the use of expensive scrapbooking equipment. Encourage everyone to bring leftover items like stickers, ribbons or colored paper for a free-for-all table.

- **Inviting retailers and consultants to participate.** Ask your local retail chains and independent supply company sales consultants to bring merchandise that can be purchased with some of the proceeds to benefit your event. They may also be willing to give brief workshops or lessons, or even help participants incorporate random

family photos into a meaningful theme.

- **Sharing scrapbooking event ideas online.** The American Cancer Society's Relay for Life community has a member forum where participants outline a variety of successful strategies for crop events to raise money for breast cancer awareness. They include tips on how and where to host events, what to charge, and how to maximize donations.

- **Pooling resources with quilters or other crafters.** If space permits, include other hobbyists who use similar tools and materials in your fundraiser. Jewelry makers, quilters, collectors and photographers are among those who may enjoy participating.

- **Supplying gift cards and generous samples.** Managers of local scrapbooking and craft stores may be eager to supply your guests with sample packs, gift cards, or generous discount coupons for lessons or supplies. Donated door prizes might include luxurious albums, high-end scissors or other tools.

Feature Fresh-air Events

Outdoor events are a nice change from the traditional gala. Go beyond the expected fundraising walks and golf tourneys to get creative in offering an outdoor event.

Consider these alternative fresh-air options to win supporters and raise funds for your library:

- ✓ **Restaurant crawl.** Donors pay a flat ticket price and walk from restaurant to restaurant sampling food and drink.
- ✓ **Concert collaboration.** Partner with a local arts charity for an outdoor performance; split costs and proceeds.
- ✓ **Big Boy Toys.** Rent backhoes, monster trucks, diggers, ATVs and dirt bikes, then let people play. Just make sure to check with your insurance provider first.

- ✓ **Field day competitions.** Include sack races, three-legged races, tug-of-war and leap-frog competitions.
- ✓ **Polar Bear Plunge.** Participants collect pledges in return for taking a dip on one of the coldest days of the year.
- ✓ **Scavenger hunts.** Instead of gathering items, people gather digital pictures of community landmarks.
- ✓ **Canoe or kayak races.**
- ✓ **Softball in the snow.**
- ✓ **Outdoor family movie night.**
- ✓ **Miniature golf tournament.**
- ✓ **Outdoor yoga event.**

Library Event Profile

Book-themed Fundraiser Writes a Success Story

An annual themed gala is helping generate major funds while engaging current and potential donors to the St. Louis Public Library Foundation (St. Louis, MO). The gala is part of the fundraising efforts for the foundation's $20 million capital campaign.

Liz Reeves, director of development and communication for the foundation, explains that in order to engage the entire community, the annual events will alternate between formal and casual ticketed events.

In November 2009, they offered a casual party that became a colorful and creative extravaganza called Stranger than Fiction: A Novel Affair. "We wanted the party to have a literary theme," says Reeves, "in order to remind people what we are working toward."

The event was an instant classic, attracting 600 guests at $75 per ticket and netting $100,000, says Reeves. She says that sticking to the event's theme proved invaluable in its success.

Specifically, she says, organizers and participants played up the literary theme by:

✓ **Dressing the part.** Guests and staff were encouraged to come dressed as their favorite literary characters. "People really went all out," says Reeves. "The costume-party feel added a lot to the atmosphere of the evening."

✓ **Spotlighting literary themes.** Five of the library's outer rooms were decorated for five genres of literature: mystery, romance, sci-fi, banned books and children's literature. The themes continued...

- **In the food** — Caterers from five restaurants were invited to present culinary takes on some classic novels: Seafood for sci-fi author Jules Verne's "20,000 Leagues Under the Sea"; Huckleberry Finn Tarts and Lady Godiva Chocolate cupcakes for banned book desserts.

- **In the drink** — A local hotel donated creative drink recipes for the cash bar: Scarlet Letter Lemonade and a Oliver's Martini, with a Twist.

- **In the entertainment** — Thematically appropriate performers were hired for each room: a marionette puppeteer in the children's literature room, an escape artist in the mystery room.

✓ **Featuring a musical interlude.** A full-sized gospel choir filled the historic, high-ceilinged marble room with music. "We wanted to remind people that we have a large collection of sheet music, scores and CDs for checkout," says Reeves.

✓ **Offering a Bookworm's Raffle.** Young volunteers went around selling raffle tickets for a unique literary privilege: to have your name used in a new book by one of several well-known authors.

✓ **Sponsoring a Shh-Silent Auction.** Including signed books, author appearances at your book club and one of 14 sets of customized Build-A-Bear Workshop plush critters, dressed to look like literary characters.

Source: Liz Reeves, Director of Development and Communication, and Mike Ryan, Development Associate, St. Louis Public Library Foundation, St. Louis, MO. E-mail: ereeves@slplfoundation.org or mryan@slplfoundation.org

Enhance Patriotic Events With Special Honors

Flags, fireworks and picnics are highlights of nearly every patriotic celebration. If you're planning a special event that will celebrate Independence Day in the United States, here are ideas to add depth and meaning to your event:

✓ **Host a concert of favorite patriotic songs.** Assemble local talent, including high school bands, soloists and ensembles to perform diverse favorites including Irving Berlin's "God Bless America" and Woody Guthrie's "This Land Is Your Land" and Julia Ward Howe's "Battle Hymn of the Republic." Choose compositions to reflect the nation's diversity with selections from the present and the past, including rock, jazz, ragtime, rhythm and blues, soul and country.

✓ **Highlight patriotic traditions of the past.** Giving the community a little advance notice, coordinate a farmer's market with produce from victory gardens inspired by World War II. Add a bake sale featuring vintage recipes to allow more people to participate in the fun.

✓ **Create and share a Hall of Heroes display.** Sponsor an exhibit of treasured military memorabilia from local families, which might include medals, photographs, uniforms or flags. Have a special area for youngsters who may be exposed to their historical significance for the first time.

✓ **Help meet a specific need for a military family.** Wounded veterans of recent conflicts in Iraq or Afghanistan often have disabilities or financial challenges. Let some of the proceeds from your event go toward a family trip, stocking their pantry or an educational fund for the veteran or his or her children.

✓ **Honor first responders in a ticker tape parade.** Firefighters, police officers and the National Guard are among those who may be called upon to do their patriotic duty at any time of day or night. Shine up their trucks, cruisers and other vehicles for a ride down Main Street led by a brass band.

Organize Brown-bag Get-togethers

Looking for a grassroots way for supporters to raise funds for your nonprofit and have fun doing it? Convince several hosts to organize brown-bag lunches at their work or home.

Get your supporters to encourage their fellow employees to pack a lunch at home and bring it to work one day a week for a month, then have them donate the money they would have spent eating out that day to your nonprofit.

Friends could also conduct brown-bag lunch fundraisers in homes. Instead of meeting friends out for lunch or dinner, they can invite them to bring a sack lunch to their home, and then donate what they would have spent eating out to your library.

Tips for Creating a Period Event

How will your event attendees know they are experiencing World War II days? How can they witness what it was like to be a part of the fabulous '50s or decadent '60s?

The atmosphere you are able to create for a period event will make a memorable experience and keep participants coming back for subsequent years' events. Here are a few helpful tips for enhancing periods in time:

- Have all workers and volunteers wear clothing of the period.
- Create a menu reminiscent of the era.
- Incorporate music — live or otherwise — that sets the mood of that time.
- Include program remarks that cite what happened "on this day in ... ."
- Select a location conducive to creating that time period.
- Be creative with the event's details — laminated newspapers of that era used as placemats, silent and live auction packages with period themes, period favors for each guest and so on.

The mood established by a special event plays an important role in determining the degree of enjoyment participants experience. Your attention to creating that mood will help distinguish your event from others.

Tips to Maximize Appeal of Food-tasting Events

The growing popularity of television's cooking competitions and celebrity chefs is feeding a growing interest in and call for food-related special events.

Along with this growing awareness of food as an entertainment venue, however, comes the demand for more than just a simple food-sampling event. Today's savvy audiences expect that you will kick it up a notch and go beyond the expected for your food-centered events.

Brainstorm with your event organizers as you review these ideas to make your food-related event a success:

- ❏ **Guess the secret ingredient**. Award a prize such as cookbooks, wine or gift baskets to guests whose palate is refined enough to determine a special spice or extract in one of the premier dishes. Who knew that fresh ginger root could liven up a simple sauce?

- ❏ **Create unique pairings on small plates**. Make your event educational by showing guests how unconventional entrees or side dishes can complement each other. Suggest wines or beverages to serve with them at home.

- ❏ **Have a cooking demonstration**. Some guests will enjoy certain foods so much they may want to prepare them for their own party. Arrange for chefs to show off their skills and entertain your audience. Provide recipes and shopping lists to take home, including any special pans or preparation tools needed for the best results.

- ❏ **Offer full-sized portions when possible**. While there may be a dozen or more selections to taste, you don't want guests to leave hungry. Be sure that reasonable quantities are available, so they can enjoy more of their favorite dishes for a full meal. If a restaurant is a sponsor of your event, ask if they will donate gift cards. If your crowd liked their offerings, they may become regular customers.

- ❏ **Arrange intimate seating areas**. This lets guests relax and discuss the foods they are enjoying. Have finger foods like raw vegetables in each area, so they can continue to eat and visit with fewer interruptions. Bring around trays with savory tidbits.

Step Up Your Game to Create Golf Tourney of Choice

Golf outings are among the top choices for fundraisers and team-building activities, so you may have to take a few extra steps to ensure that yours will be the one donors and supporters choose to attend.

Set your golf event apart from the rest with one or more of these elements:

- ❑ **Lessons from a pro.** Give participants several chances to get some tips on improving swing, flexibility, and how and when to use hitting irons and woods. Offer lessons for several skill levels.

- ❑ **Give a useful gift to each participant.** Think newly released golfing biography or instruction book, set of golf balls with your logo, ball markers, divot tools, all-in-one caddies and statistics tracker notebooks.

- ❑ **Include family activities for non-golfers.** Create a family-friendly venue by including swimming, a fireworks display, picnic dinner near the greens, children's putting contests or scenic cart rides.

- ❑ **Hold a hole-in-one contest.** Increase participation by holding prequalifying rounds at local driving ranges with a charge per shot. Buy insurance to cover the cost of prizes up to $1 million if an entrant makes a hole-in-one.

- ❑ **Get sponsors for each hole.** Eighteen or more sponsors mean more prizes, activities and participants, increased revenue and greater media exposure.

- ❑ **Offer passes for each day of your tournament.** One-day passes to the golf facilities, restaurants and discounts at the pro shop let non-golfers mingle with participating friends and allow them to attend on the most convenient day.

- ❑ **Corporate hospitality packages.** Involve businesses in your event by offering packages that include special passes, food or merchandise discounts or admission to related festivities during the tournament.

- ❑ **Offer marketing opportunities for every budget.** From a skybox area to a coupon for a free pizza in goodie bags, be open to creative and cost-effective ways for big and small businesses to be a part of your event. They get positive exposure, and your participants get more perks.

Update Your Yearly Golf Event

Some annual events fade as years go by, not because they aren't popular, but because they get stale. To keep your annual golf event vibrant, add new features each year.
Here are ideas for doing so:

- ✓ Create A and B flights, so golfers compete only against those at their level.

- ✓ Have a celebrity impersonator (e.g., Marilyn Monroe, Bill Clinton) or a local celebrity (mayor, TV news anchor) greet golfers on the fourth green.

- ✓ Add new prizes: 1st and 2nd place net and gross in each flight.

- ✓ Make a commemorative gift to golfers on your event's milestone anniversary (e.g., 10th anniversary).

- ✓ Have everyone use the same special putter on the 12th green.

- ✓ Play a video of golf bloopers during the social hour.

For That Next Golf Event ...

Looking for a unique prize for your golf fundraiser? Try this:

Convince a local car dealer to donate a demonstration car for your closest-to-the-pin winner. Whoever wins gets to drive the car displayed for a weekend of their choice at no cost to you or to the dealer.

A win for everyone, this great advertising for the car dealer also gets the winner in the car dealership.

Include a Collector's Item With Annual Special Events

If you host a repeat event year after year, be sure to include some sort of collector item that attendees will receive (or purchase) as a keepsake.
A sampling of examples might include:

- A button with a winning design selected by a panel of judges. (The button could serve as ticket the to the event.)

- A limited-edition holiday ornament, seasonal print or artwork.

- A photograph taken with each year's event celebrity.

- A book signed by the author.

- A handwritten note from someone served by your organization — one note per attendee, each different.

Annual collector items add to the fun and provide one more reason for attendees to keep coming back year after year.

Library Event Profile

Organization's Theme Ties Into Event

Each year, Literacy Instruction for Texas (LIFT) of Dallas, TX, works to engage and support nearly 8,500 adult learners in their quest for literacy. For 48 years, LIFT has been enhancing lives through literacy by orchestrating 157 classes at 15 sites taught by more than 500 volunteers each week.

To celebrate and support the organization's efforts, the organization hosts an annual Champions of Literacy Luncheon, which draws some 300 people a year.

Tahra Taylor, interim executive director, answers questions about the event:

How are funds raised at the event? How much was raised at the most recent event?

"Prior to the event, we raised funds through table sponsorships and individual ticket sales. At the event, we raised funds by selling individual tickets at the door, raffle tickets for prizes, and autographed copies of the speaker's books. Our last event raised approximately $48,000 after expenses."

In what ways do you honor literacy at the event?

"At the September 2009 event, world-renowned mystery author Deborah Crombie was the keynote speaker and she generously agreed to allow LIFT to include the naming of a character in her next book as a raffle prize. Other ways that we tie in literacy to the event is to hold the event in September during National Literacy month and select a theme tied to literacy. Our theme last year was LIFT Off With Books, and the luncheon was held at the Frontiers of Flight Museum in Dallas. We also select one of our adult learners to read his or her story and show a video about LIFT to demonstrate the impact of our programs in the lives of our students and future generations. Last year we used decorated stacks of books as centerpieces and the centerpiece was given to a guest at each table."

At the 2008 event, you were looking for signed books from authors of all genres — how did you use those books?

"In 2008 we received over 300 books. This year we received three book titles without sending a formal request. These books were included in baskets we assembled for raffle items."

What is your best tip for locating authors and getting them to donate signed copies to a fundraising event?

"My best tip is to send the author a request for donated signed copies of his or her book(s). I also suggest asking board members, volunteers and donors if they are aware of authors who might donate one or more of their books for the event."

Source: Tahra Taylor, Interim Executive Director, Literacy Instruction for Texas, Dallas, TX. E-mail: ttaylor@lift-texas.org

Make Hats Part of Your Event

Napoleon, Abraham Lincoln, Jacqueline Kennedy Onassis and Charlie Chaplin are just a few famous people known for their trademark hats.

Your organization can also celebrate hats by including the accessories as part of a special event. You could even create a new event that's sure to generate opportunities for photos and media coverage by placing hats center stage.

Here are ideas to get you started:

✓ **Use hats as centerpieces.** Hats can be integrated into nearly any event or holiday theme for any age group. Hats from children's books like Madeline or Dr. Seuss, sports figures, film stars or fictional characters like Sherlock Holmes are just a few options.

✓ **Offer hats off to your supporters.** Order baseball caps, stocking caps, cowboy hats, knit beanies or other popular styles to give as party favors at your next fundraiser. Visors or ball caps work for summer events, cowboy hats are popular for barbecues, and knit styles go over well for wintertime events.

✓ **Pair international hats and food.** Mexican sombreros, French berets, Spanish matador styles and the Greek fez not only inspire themes and decorations, but also help determine menu possibilities.

✓ **Sponsor a hat-themed contest.** Think of the "different hats" your organization wears in the community, and hold a contest for supporters to create hats that match each facet of your mission to wear to your event.

✓ **Plan a hat costume party.** Full costume balls are fun, but the effort they take may discourage some supporters from attending. People can usually find or create fascinating hats to match attire they already planned to wear. So send out invitations for a hat costume party in which people don chapeaus that reflect certain characters or celebrities.

✓ **Hold a hat auction.** Donors can supply hats of all styles, shapes, historical significance or price range for you to auction as part of your event. Winning bidders can enjoy wearing their purchases for the rest of the event.

Fundraising for Libraries: How to Plan Profitable Special Events.
Edited by Scott C. Stevenson.
© 2012 Stevenson, Inc. Published 2012 by Stevenson, Inc.

Fundraising for Libraries: How to Plan Profitable Special Events

Revenue-generating Components

Too many special events fall far short of what could have been generated in revenue simply because no one was willing to consider other revenue-generating ideas that often times don't require that much extra effort. Explore every revenue-generating strategy possible — ticket sales, sponsorships, live/silent auctions, raffles, donations, advertising in a printed program and more — to raise additional funds.

Get Your Special Event Attendees in the Bidding Mood

When live auctions are part of your gala fundraiser, you have two major challenges: finding desirable, big-ticket items from donors and getting your audience in the right bidding mood.

So many variables impact patrons' feelings while the auction is in progress:

✓ Did they enjoy their dinner and believe it was worth the ticket price?

✓ Is the room well-lit and comfortable?

✓ Are the registration and bidding processes simple to understand and unintimidating for newcomers?

✓ Are acoustics good enough that the auctioneer can be heard?

Consider these issues as you begin planning your special event:

- **'Tis it the season to be jolly?** Auctions during the end-of-year holiday season can be iffy for several reasons. People may be feeling tapped out financially and emotionally from gift shopping or uneasy about year-end financial reports. At the same time, people may feel especially generous at this heartwarming time of year. Take a look at your area's overall economy and determine if it has affected your supporters for the better. Spring might be a better time for a fundraiser when most people are feeling optimistic and upbeat.

- **Find a personable auctioneer or celebrity.** A local notable, or one of your most colorful staff or board members, may be a good choice. A team of two can be effective, too, especially if the guests enjoy the chemistry between them.

- **Keep it short and sweet.** By offering fewer, but higher-quality items, participants won't be as likely to be scanning the program to see how far down the list you are, and how many more items are left before they can exit gracefully.

- **Show the audience the goods.** A fur coat or diamond ring are very portable, and a young model can easily stroll through the tables during the bidding to show interested parties the merchandise and let them try it on or touch it. Purebred puppies are another auction favorite that should be seen and enjoyed while the auction is

taking place.

- **Set the mood for each item.** Have appropriate music or dance to introduce each attraction. A hula dancer for a Hawaiian vacation, a singing cowboy for a trip to the Grand Canyon or a chorus girl for a Las Vegas getaway make the auction seem more like an entertaining show.

- **Advertise the most desirable selections before the event.** When you mail the invitations, design an attractive insert to show guests some of the exciting possibilities: a limited edition work of art, a brand-new, fully loaded vehicle, an exotic piece of gemstone jewelry from a famous store or collectible autographed items can build anticipation and help guests plan which items most interest them — serious buyers will come prepared, and if they are outbid, they may console themselves with their second choice!

- **Ask popular contributors to act as spotters.** If a guest's friends are milling about keeping track of bids, they may bid more quickly when cajoled and encouraged by someone they like and know well. Good-natured competition, moderated by a friendly third party, can result in record high donations while a good time is being had by all.

> **Winning Event Tip**
>
> ■ For those who can't attend your event, ask for a contribution to sponsor others' attendance — employees, clients, volunteers, students, etc.

- **Be sure guests can see all merchandise before the event.** Let them sit in cars, try on furs and jewelry, or play with exotic pets before bidding begins, as well as during the auction. Few buyers will offer significant amounts for merchandise they can't (at least partially) evaluate or see a practical use for in their lives.

The level of collective enthusiasm plays a key role in an auction's bidding process. These strategies will help to maximize the liveliness of your crowd and get them active in supporting your efforts through the auction.

Silent Auctions Are Easy and Profitable

A silent auction can add spark and profits to your event. Even if you have no experience with this activity, you can be successful. Try these tips:

Acquire auction items through various means:

- Solicit donations from businesses and offer publicity in return.
- Buy additional auction items on sale and add value by packaging them with other items.
- Gift certificates for services (e.g., house cleaning, pet sitting, a homemade pie each month for a year) make great auction fare.
- Inspire competition among those soliciting items with a contest for best gift package.

Dress up your auction items:

- Eye candy is the byword at silent auctions. Visually desirable displays draw higher bids.
- Bundle related items (bubble bath, candles, lotion) in stunning baskets.
- Accessorize small pieces. Display jewelry in a crystal box on a silk scarf.
- Exhibit gift certificates, such as a spa visit, on quality embroidered towels.

Think through the bidding process in advance:

- Prepare a bid sheet detailing the offering (e.g., limo ride and dinner for two at Captain Jack's).
- For public bidding, have participants record their name/number and the dollar amount bid on bid sheets next to each item, allowing guests to view the earlier bids.
- For anonymity, assign guests a bid number to put next to their bid, or have them place their name and top bid on a slip of paper deposited in a container.
- At a set time, announce the winning bidder of each item.

Inspire Additional Auction Gifts

Reward the biggest spender — Announce that the person who spends the most on silent auction purchases will earn a private dinner with your library board chair or head librarian.

Stimulate competition and spending — A contest for most attractive basket or best silent auction display can bring additional donations. Place a secure container or assign a volunteer to each basket. Each dollar placed in the container counts as a vote. At event end, count the dollars and honor the winning entry.

Make it easy to spend money — Let attendees know in advance that you accept credit cards to encourage higher bids.

Pump Up Your Silent Auction

Silent auctions are popular and successful ways to raise funds as part of gala events because big-ticket items are often donated, meaning pure profit for your organization.

But too much of a good thing can cause difficulties: more items than buyers, too much traffic around the silent auction display, and lower-quality offerings.

For a profitable, enjoyable silent auction:

1. **Choose items carefully.** Be discriminating in approaching donors, asking only those likely to give an item that is attractive, useful and desirable to a large cross section of guests. For instance, a generous gift certificate from a popular restaurant good for a year may bring a far better return than a July week in a time-share condo in Vail.

2. **Less is better.** If your event includes a live auction for big-ticket items, keep your silent auction smaller. Thirty to 50 quality items will be enough for guests to have a good selection. Group similar items into themed packages.

3. **Enlist your best volunteer buyer.** If one of your volunteers has experience as a gift shop buyer, worked in a retail environment or even owned a specialty store, ask him/her to serve on the silent auction committee for acquisitions and/or display. His/her skills will make your auction area organized, attractive and user-friendly.

4. **Consider the season.** Will guests be shopping for holiday gifts or stretched to the limit after Christmas bills arrive? Keep traditional consumer spending habits in mind and plan your silent auction for peak buying times.

5. **Vary donors from auction to auction.** If your contingency of supporters is consistent about attending your events, they may grow weary of seeing similar items donated by the same contributors. Ask different artists, jewelers, furriers, travel agencies and restaurants each time, unless their donations are always in demand.

6. **Be sure your display area is large, well-lit and easy to negotiate.** This helps avoid congestion, spilled drinks, accidents and difficulty viewing items. Leave plenty of room for clearly marked bid sheets and for posting auction rules so bidders can easily find all items — especially the one's that drew them to the event in the first place.

Library Event Profile

Electronic Silent Auction Technology Boosts Event

For more than 20 years, the Dinner in the Stacks annual fundraiser at the Burton Barr Central Library (Phoenix, AZ) has been a staple of the area's social calendar, raising hundreds of thousands of dollars for literacy programs and other worthy causes.

Staged by The Phoenix Public Library Foundation (Phoenix, AZ), the event is the library's premier annual fundraiser. It features components such as a cocktail hour, silent auction and dinner.

The 2010 event drew 600 attendees, netted more than $200,000 and added a high-tech twist.

Foundation Director Geraldine Hills says the event's silent auction went to an electronic format in 2010. Foundation officials worked with IML Worldwide, which provided hand-held devices that guests used to bid on the silent auction items.

The use of the hand-held devices allowed the bidding to stay open longer and let guests post Twitter messages, egging each other on and driving up the bids. On average, Hills says, the electronic format has the potential to increase proceeds by 35 percent, though the silent auction at the 2010 event saw significantly less growth, reflecting challenges common to all Phoenix-based events.

During the program, guests were also given the chance to use their bidding devices to make pledges. Volunteers were in place to work with guests who needed help with the high-tech devices.

For the 2011 event, organizers planned to add an online component where people could bid on silent auction items remotely if they couldn't attend the fundraiser. Changes to the configuration of the event were possible as well, Hills says, thanks to added flexibility from the electronic format of the silent auction.

The Phoenix Public Library Foundation was also considering expanding changes to the event for 2011, moving to a food station, multiple-activity event rather than the formal sit-down dinner. Hill says, "The electronic format would allow for this restructuring and greater use of the library for the event."

Source: Geraldine Hills, Director, The Phoenix Public Library Foundation, Phoenix, AZ. E-mail: Geraldine.Hills@phoenix.gov

Tips for Orchestrating The Best Silent Auction

Silent auctions are a tried-and-true method of bringing necessary funds into nonprofit organizations. But success doesn't just happen. To gain the most positive publicity and proceeds from your next silent auction, try the following tips for success:

- **Spotlight your main items.** Using well-placed lighting can help emphasize your big-ticket items at your silent auction. Use picture lights, spotlights or fine art lighting to emphasize and feature your main items to draw the bidders to that item. Ask a local museum or curator for advice and tips.

- **Prominently place silent auction items.** Be sure to put silent auction items near a high traffic area to get the most exposure to bidding guests such as near the ticket booth, refreshment area or even the bathrooms.

- **Style clothing.** If your silent auction includes clothing, use mannequins to display these items. Add accessories such as hat, purses and jewelry to complete the look and include them with the auction item.

- **Create and share detailed descriptions.** Ask the writer among your volunteers to come up with well-written and detailed descriptions for the items.

- **Think location, location, location.** Place the most valuable items in the most prominent areas with the most foot traffic to generate the most buzz and, ultimately, bidding.

- **Create and circulate silent auction announcements.** It's important that the event host for the evening announces when silent auction items are up for bid and should offer guests a countdown until close of that item. Allow ample time for guests to make their way to the bid sheet in order to maximize on the number of bidders. Announce the close of the item and have someone on hand to pull the bid sheet.

Plan Ahead to Avoid Top 10 Auction Mistakes

Do you have a silent, live or online auction planned as part of your library's next special event? Don't let all your auction preparation time, gift solicitation, organization and packaging go to waste because of simple, avoidable mistakes.

Charity auctioneer Lance Walker, who conducts some 100 fundraising auctions and workshops for charities throughout North America each year, cites the Top 10 mistakes made by event planners:

10. Not having the all auctions in the same room.

9. Poor item display and not using slides or video to spotlight items during the auction.

8. Poor lighting. Brighter is better.

7. Using small bid numbers or not using bid numbers at all.

6. Closing the silent booths before dinner. Keeping them open holds people longer, increases profits and helps keep attendees entertained.

5. Starting the live auction too late or not on time. With 20 items or less, start later than usual.

4. Not having enough energetic spotters to catch bids and keep the mood lively.

3. Beginning the live auction after the sit-down dinner is over. People are at their best while eating.

2. Using an insufficient sound system. Use at least four large speakers on stands in each corner.

1. Not utilizing a dynamic professional fundraising auctioneer. Don't wait until the last minute to line up this key player.

"Many other mistakes can and are made," Walker contends, "but auctions continue to be a great way to raise consistent revenue and promote goodwill among constituents."

Source: Lance Walker, Walker Auctions, Germantown, TN. E-mail: lance@walkerauctions.com.

Five Basket Ideas for Your Silent Auction

One of the single best ways to increase revenue on donations of smaller items to your silent auction is to group them together in baskets or packages. Here are some of the most popular:

- **Gone to the Dogs.** Fill this basket with gift certificates for boarding, grooming or doggie day care and certificates to pet shops or big box pet stores. Chew toys, treats and other small items like leashes and collars can be included. Depending on the time of year and type of event you may also want to include a doggie Halloween costume or Christmas outfit. A Diva Dog basket could include many of the same things with higher-end canine couture items and organic treats. And a My Dog and Me basket could include pampering for both dog and owner, with certificates for pet grooming and a relaxing mani-pedi for mom.

- **A Baker's Dozen.** This basket includes 13 unique or coveted pieces/tools for any baker's kitchen, along with gift certificates to specialty food stores or a local baking challenge. Also make sure to include a recipe book or two.

- **Up All Night.** This basket should include items to pamper new parents, and could include anything from bottles of wine to eye masks. Other ideas include gift certificates for take-out meals or food prep kitchens, massages or pedicures and house cleaning or laundry services. If it will make a new parent's life easier, it should be in this basket.

- **The Busy Executive.** Good items to include in this basket might be gift certificates for a round of golf, upscale restaurants or even a concierge service.

- **Holiday Baskets.** A trim-your-tree basket could include upscale or one-of-a-kind ornaments and a handmade tree skirt, along with a bottle of wine, snacks and a holiday music CD to make decorating the tree more fun. Fourth of July might be a picnic basket filled with lawn games, sparklers, bubble wands and a blanket.

Know Silent Auction Gift Ramifications

If your library's fundraising event uses silent auctions to raise money, keep these tips in mind:

1. Include the items' **fair market values** on bid sheets and programs. If the value is not listed prior to the start of the auction, whatever is bid on the item is considered by the IRS to be the value. This means there is no charitable deduction, even if someone bids thousands of dollars more than the known value.

2. Receipts for **charitable deductions** need to list the fair market value and total bid. The IRS only considers the amount paid over the value as a charitable deduction.

3. If any items have **restrictions** — such as days allowed for golf or hotel stays — or if anything is excluded from the donation (e.g., installation costs), include that information in the program, on bid sheets and on any gift certificates for the items.

4. Determine before the auction how you will **follow up** with donors, buyers and volunteers after the event is over. Things to include in your plans are sending thank-you letters to donors, contacting buyers who didn't pick up their items, sending flowers to volunteers and fulfilling other stewardship steps. How you handle things after the event can set the stage for how successful you'll be the next time.

Presentation Key to Silent Auction Success

We all know that the tickets, passes or certificates are the real value of the silent auction item. Yet human beings appreciate beauty, appearance and presentation, and two tickets sitting on a table leave quite a bit to be desired.

Why ask your supporters to imagine the experience, when, by adding a few small details, you could evoke that experience for them in vivid detail? The following are just a few examples of what this might look like in practice:

- Two tickets to a college football game could be augmented with a university-branded ball and commemorative magazine or publication celebrating the team's recent season or successes. A small gift certificate to a specialty meat shop could be included, if a tailgate is involved.

- A gift certificate to a high-end winery could be paired with a few take-home bottles (they need not be expensive), an elegant pair of wine glasses and a bouquet of flowers adorned with an assortment of corks.

- A week at a condo in the Florida Keys could be turned into an extravaganza of tropical fruits and flowers, possibly on a bed of sand and shells. A travel guide describing the island would add interest and prove useful to the eventual recipient.

These ancillary items might seem small, and indeed, they will usually add almost nothing to the cost of the item. Yet the impact they can have on potential buyers should not be overlooked — nor should their impact on the bottom line of your silent auction.

Increase Revenue, Sell More Chinese Auction Tickets

Revenue from ticket sales will make or break your Chinese auction, so finding ways to increase that revenue is imperative. Try using the following tips to boost your success:

- **Sell tickets in advance.** Chinese auctions rely heavily on how many people attend the event, but selling tickets in advance allows you to reach out to people who may be on the fence about attending. Giving them the chance to purchase tickets in advance, at a discount, may get them off the fence. If tickets normally cost $1 each, offer them for $0.75 each, if people purchase them in advance. You can also offer discounts and incentives for bigger ticket bundles.

- **Make way for those who can't attend.** Find a way for your constituents who can't attend the event to participate. Send a list of the items that will be auctioned

and let them mail their purchased tickets back in with their preferences. If you feel that this may cause a problem with those who do attend, have a limited number of items available for bidding by those not in attendance.

- **Use social media.** Though Chinese auctions have been around a long time, technology can breathe new life into your event. Use Facebook and Twitter to announce what items will be available to bid on, complete with pictures. Consider offering a weekly prize to the person who prepays for the most tickets or the volunteer who secures the most prize donations. Generate excitement for the contests through Tweets. Let the winner pick something from your organization's inventory. In addition to increasing ticket sales it will also boost awareness.

Library Event Profile

Library's Annual Appeal Generates $20,000

The math is so simple, any nonprofit in need of annual funding could do it: 12 volunteers + 12 phones + 2 evenings = $20,000.

The Malvern Public Library (Malvern, PA) has been holding an annual phonathon for the past 20 years. "We feel this is a very easy way to fundraise. For almost no overhead or out-of-pocket expense, we raised $20,000 this year," says Rosalie Dietz, director of the library.

Calls are made from 6:30 p.m. to 8:45 p.m. on a Sunday and Monday, usually in late March or early April. "We have settled on late winter/early spring because it works with our schedule and it seems to be a time when most people are still at home in the early evening. We avoid the Easter holiday, because schools are closed and families go on vacation," Dietz says.

What does it take to have a successful phonathon?

- **A large database.** The library maintains a database of about 450 names. It's made up of many past donors and new library members. "Each year we focus on a different part of our service area and call patrons from those areas who have not donated in the past. We try to expand the list each year, and we've been marginally increasing our total," says Dietz.

- **A print out.** Each volunteer caller is given a sheet with the name, address, phone number and the past four-year's donation history of the people they will be calling.

- **Pre-printed "Thank you for making a pledge ..." and "Sorry we missed you ..." letters.** "We work in teams, one person makes the call, and one person serves as scribe addressing envelopes," says Dietz. This utilizes those volunteers who are not comfortable asking for money, which is a necessity for maximizing volunteer participation.

- **Multiple phone lines.** If multiple lines aren't available at your organization, see if you could set up the phonathon in a nearby school or ask your volunteer callers if they would be willing to use their own cell phone.

This year the library also did a pre-phonathon appeal to local businesses. Those businesses were then recognized in all the phonathon mailings.

Once the phonathon begins, Dietz has found that the majority of the pledges come on the first night. Those supporters who don't answer on Sunday are called again on Monday. If they still don't answer, they are mailed a "Sorry we missed you ..." letter. "By the end of the second night we have hand-addressed thank-you and missed-you letters ready to go," Dietz says.

Since most volunteers bring their own cell phones to use and the postage to mail thank-you and missed-you letters is donated by a local bank, the only cost the library must pay is a light dinner for the volunteers.

Source: Rosalie Dietz, Director, Malvern Public Library, Malvern, PA. E-mail: rdietz@ccls.org

Make Sure Volunteers Know What to Say

Before your phonathon volunteers pick up the phone, make sure they know what to say when the person on the other end answers. At the Malvern Public Library (Malvern, PA) a sample dialogue is provided to volunteers before the phonathon begins and instructs them to:

- Introduce themselves and identify their relationship with the library.

- Explain where the funds will go.

- Tell the donor what they donated last year and ask if they can increase their donation this year.

- Ask if the donor would like to designate a person to honor with a bookplate if the donation is for $50 or more.

- Mention matching funds from employers if available.

Maximize Auction Mileage

Begin an annual tradition.

Next time you're planning that live or silent auction for your special event, be sure to include one item that is up for purchase and then returned at the end of one year for the next auction.

Examples: Keys to a second residence donated for a week each year or an engraved champagne glass plus several bottles of bubbly.

Fundraising for Libraries: How to Plan Profitable Special Events

Maximizing Sponsorship Revenue

Sponsorships are a big part of most special events. At a minimum, sponsorships can underwrite your events' costs so every dollar you generate in other ways becomes profit. At their best, sponsorships can generate thousands of dollars in net income, attract guests and build greater awareness of your library and its value to the public. Make sponsorships a key component of your event planning process. The partnerships you form with event sponsors will oftentimes extend far beyond the life of the event.

Seven Unique Benefits to Offer Event Sponsors

The logo on the event program, the banner on the website, the complimentary set of VIP tickets — you know the kinds of benefits businesses are always offered in return for sponsorship support and chances are they do, too.

There's nothing wrong with these tried-and-true perks, but offering a few new twists might make your event stand out among potential sponsors. Consider the following for a few new ideas:

1. **Event status designations.** Your event has moral and/or professional weight. Use that influence by offering potential sponsors the opportunity to earn a preferred supplier status, or to give one of their products an official product status (e.g, official running shoe of a marathon, official wireless provider of a conference).

2. **On-site display opportunities.** Your event will be bringing together a large number of people around a narrow theme. This can be a golden opportunity for the right businesses. Let them conduct on-site sampling, demonstrations and/or displays in return for generous sponsorship support.

3. **Access to talent.** Celebrities will attract participants to your event, but they will also be a draw for sponsors. Offer access to your well-known headliners, whether through private meetings or exclusive events held with key staff or clients, as part of your benefit package.

4. **Database marketing.** The database generated by your event's registration process might be of great interest to potential sponsors. Consider giving access to it for a company's direct mail initiatives, but offer this benefit only sparingly. You don't want to drive people away from your event with a flood of unsolicited mail.

5. **Employment recruiting.** Businesses are always looking for the best and the brightest, and your event might be just the place to find them. Give select sponsors the opportunity to set up a staff recruitment display and/or distribute recruitment information.

6. **Proof-of-purchase promotion.** Looking to woo retail-oriented sponsors? Help drive business their way by discounting admission, parking or merchandise at your event with proof of purchase from their stores.

7. **Charitable support.** Businesses look at the bottom line, but that's not always the only thing they look at. Socially conscious companies might be attracted by an offer to involve the sponsor's chosen charity in the event or donate a small portion of ticket sales to it.

Attract, Reward Event Sponsors With Varied Benefits

As you promote various types of sponsorship opportunities for your special event, create a checklist of possibilities, knowing benefits will be perceived differently among would-be sponsors.

Here are some examples of possible sponsor benefits to offer:

❑ Logo visibility in promotional ads and materials.

❑ Complimentary event/program admission for employees.

❑ On-site visibility through signage.

❑ On-site product placement, giveaway and sampling opportunities.

❑ VIP and courtesy passes.

❑ Access to event planning services.

❑ Speaking and naming opportunities.

❑ Recognition in publications and on your website.

❑ Complimentary copies of particular publications.

❑ Branded merchandise.

❑ Opportunity to host private receptions.

❑ Opportunity to host exclusive tours.

❑ Special seating/parking privileges.

❑ Access to member names/addresses.

❑ Specialized publicity.

Invite Sponsors to a Preview Party

To justify higher price tags for sponsorship opportunities, invite all sponsors to a preview party for your special event as an extra benefit. Special touches for preview party attendees might include:

- Valet (or preferred) parking. Pre-bid opportunities on auction items.
- Distinctive name tags.
- A corsage or boutonniere.
- Up-close contact with a celebrity.
- Champagne.

Get Sponsorship Costs Covered

Here's an idea to get costs associated with sponsorship covered:

Identify 11 businesses each capable of giving $1,000. Approach each with an invitation to sponsor the event you have identified as worthy of its support.

Use 10 of the $1,000 gifts to generate $10,000 in needed revenue and the 11th to underwrite benefits for all 11 sponsors (e.g., advertising costs you would normally have to pay that publicize the sponsors).

Put Sponsorships on the Table

Sponsorships can make or break a special event.

Many company leaders find table sponsorship attractive if the sponsorship gives them marketing value and lets them reward customers, shareholders and employees with tickets to the event.

When creating an appealing table sponsorship package, consider:

- **Will table sponsorships be separate or part of larger sponsorship packages?** Having packages just for tables allows you to sell more of them and target companies that might not be able to afford general event sponsorship. Having a table as a complementary part of general sponsorships is a nice perk for larger sponsors.

- **What will table sponsors receive in return?** This depends on how much you want to raise through the sponsorships. If table sponsorship cost is relatively low (e.g., just above or below ticket cost multiplied by number of seats), returns would be minimal. You might offer recognition in promotions and on event signage. If sponsorship cost is higher, add perks such as V.I.P. seating and verbal recognition during the program.

- **Logistics.** Think through details beforehand. Selling too many corporate tables might not seem like a problem until you realize you have no seats left for important donors. Premier seating is not a perk if blocked by a sound system or light pole.

Recruit Table Captains

Recruit table captains for your event. Their sole responsibility: to fill tables.

Choose persons well-versed and passionate about what your organization does. They should have a comfort level with the ask since the job is really all about selling.

Whether they bring in corporate tables or individual seats doesn't really matter, as long as they meet their set goal, which you should discuss with them ahead of time.

Recognize Your Event's Corporate Sponsors

You have the good fortune to have a noted corporate sponsor for your next event. Showcasing your partnership helps elevate esteem for both of you. Consider these approaches for involving them in as many high profile ways as possible:

- ✓ **Name a major service award for the corporation.** If your event includes recognizing key people in your organization, ask the corporate CEO to present the "XYZ Company Spirit Award" to a top honoree.

- ✓ **Ask company staff to be judges or announcers.** Your event may have scholarship presentations, prize drawings, an art show with awards or a major auction item. Be sure representatives from the corporation are front and center when all eyes are on that activity.

- ✓ **Widely use the company logo.** Include the sponsor logo in backdrops, on napkins and nametags, on decorations and in floral arrangements. Athletic events offer opportunities with T-shirts, water bottles or wristbands.

- ✓ **Ask them to help you identify ways to promote them.** The direct approach can be the most effective. A brainstorming session with the corporate sponsor's communications staff may uncover some fresh strategies that will come from two distinct viewpoints — theirs and yours.

- ✓ **Use their facility for your event.** Your sponsor may have wide green lawns, a spacious atrium, auditorium or dining facility that is ideal for your occasion. More than simply asking that they underwrite food and beverage costs, give them the chance to open their doors and introduce themselves to the community.

- ✓ **Include them in public service announcements (PSAs).**

Dos and Don'ts to Boost Your Sponsorship Revenue

Corporate sponsorship is one of the largest single sources of revenue in special event and program-based fundraising. It is also one of the most volatile, capable of fluctuating widely from year to year — both up and down.

Winning the support of corporate partners requires mutual trust and a close alignment of interests, but a few time-tested pointers can make a big difference for your library. To help you make the most of your outreach efforts, Jean Block, president of Jean Block Consulting Inc. (Albuquerque, NM), offers the following lists of sponsorship solicitation dos and don'ts.

DON'T:

- Address a request to "Dear Friend." Do your homework and find out who should receive your request.
- Ask the Right Sponsor for the Wrong Thing. Research the sponsor's priorities.
- Ask the Right Sponsor at the Wrong Time. Research their giving cycles.
- Whine at the companies who turn you down. Instead, politely ask them for suggestions on how to improve your proposal.
- Be too busy to write thank-you letters (especially creative ones).
- Assume you are the only one asking. Develop a way to show how you are different from or better than other nonprofits.
- Toss the sponsor's guidelines aside and submit only what you want. There are reasons for the sponsor's questions.
- Go around the person whose responsibility it is to deal with your request.
- Only contact the sponsor when you want money.
- Keep calling — constantly — to check on the progress of your proposal.

DO:

- Look for ways to collaborate with other organizations if you can. Combine your requests for higher impact.
- Seize an opportunity to follow up with sponsors. Send a quarterly progress report and get them involved in the success of your event.
- Ask the sponsor how to show your appreciation. Be sure that you deliver what you promise. Take pictures. Value the sponsor's investment.
- Make a personal visit to the potential sponsor before a significant request; take an influential board member or volunteer. Interview the sponsor, ask questions and listen to the sponsor's requests.
- Be creative with your request. Money isn't the only thing sponsors have to offer. Look for in-kind opportunities.
- Give more than adequate leadtime for the sponsor to respond to your request. Research giving cycles.
- Thank the potential sponsor for their consideration, even if you are turned down. Remember that you are building a relationship for the future.
- Ask for references of other sponsors who might be interested in your program or project.
- Do a quality control check. Be sure you have spelled the sponsor's name correctly, have the right title, address, etc.

Block, who spent years on the corporate side of corporate philanthropy, says these steps may sound simple, but they can have a powerful effect on your fundraising efforts. Following these simple steps, she says, will distinguish your organization from the great majority of nonprofit sponsorship-seekers and help you secure much-needed sponsorship dollars.

Source: Jean Block, President, Jean Block Consulting Inc., Albuquerque, NM.
E-mail: jean@jblockinc.com

Offer Sponsor Perks

- To make your event's sponsors feel even more special, arrange to have them picked up and dropped off at your event in a limousine.

Don't Overlook Sponsors' Employees

Anytime you convince a business to step forward and help sponsor an event, be sure to involve their employees as well. Examples include:

- Selling tickets
- Delivering drinks
- Setting up and cleaning up
- Hosting and greeting
- Conducting tours
- Transportation and parking
- Registration
- Answering phones

You may even see opportunities to incorporate fun competition and prizes into employees' involvement.

Library Event Profile

Theme, Sponsorship Key to Library Fundraiser

You've probably heard of the bestselling book "Eat, Pray, Love," but how about the fundraising event Eat, Play, Read to benefit a home to books, The Ferguson Library (Stamford, CT)?

"The event was our first ever fundraiser here at the library," says Communications Supervisor Linda Avellar. "We had recently completed a renovation of the main library and wanted to hold the event there, since many people in the community hadn't been in the building since the renovation. The concept Eat, Play, Read was a play on the popular book/film "Eat, Pray, Love," and was meant to be fun and a little whimsical. I think we achieved that with the evening we put together."

A dozen local restaurants and caterers donated food and set up tables to offer tastings. One of the town's major liquor stores donated wine, scotch and beer for tastings, as well as an open bar, reducing event costs tremendously. A jazz band played throughout the evening, while guests enjoyed a live auction and organized tours of the library. Those who participated in the tours were eligible for a raffle at the end of the evening. Avellar says, "It was a great way to get people around the building, and people were thrilled with the tours."

People also enjoyed the fact that the library, an elegant building with soaring ceilings and a grand staircase, was used as the venue.

Avellar says the event's intent was to be both a fundraiser and a friend-raiser. "We hoped to engage the entire Stamford community, especially those who might not be regular library users. We sustained a $1.2 million budget cut this year and were forced to scale back services and reduce hours system wide. Eat, Play, Read was an effort to raise funds and educate the community about what we do. On both accounts, we believe the evening was a big success."

The event raised approximately $100,000. Avellar says they had a robust response from individuals at every level of sponsorship. "We had 38 sponsors total, ranging from $500 to $25,000. The depth of the response was very encouraging." Indeed, it accounted for the majority of revenue raised.

Revenue was also generated through ticket sales, a live auction and a giving tree.

Source: Linda Avellar, Communications Supervisor, The Ferguson Library, Stamford, CT. Phone (203) 351-8208. E-mail: linda@fergusonlibrary.org

The success of the Eat, Play Read event of The Ferguson Library depended in large part on sponsorship revenue. Shown here is the event-specific sponsorship form organizers used to raise donations of up to $25,000.

Content not available in this edition

Boost Sponsorship Revenue

To increase the number of event sponsors for your organization and increase existing sponsors' level of support, create a ladder of sponsorship opportunities.

Develop a list of all available sponsorship opportunities arranged in least- to most-expensive order. Each increasing level should obviously include more attractive benefits for the would-be sponsor.

When calling on new prospects, offer less-costly sponsorship opportunities to get them on board with your organization. Invite those with a history of sponsorships to a higher level with more exclusive benefits.

This laddering method will help you add new sponsors and move existing sponsors toward increased levels of support.

Fundraising for Libraries: How to Plan Profitable Special Events

Strive for Record-breaking Attendance

Whether your library's goal is to make new friends, raise the public's awareness of your library and its programs, to generate needed funds for your library or a combination of all three, getting guests to attend your event is the bottom line. And as much time and effort as it takes to pull off an event, why not do all you can to maximize its attendance? The examples and strategies shared here will help to attract the highest number of participants for your library's next event.

Create a Plan to Beat Last Year's Attendance

If you repeat a particular fundraising event each year, how much time do you put into setting attendance goals designed to surpass the previous years' numbers? That key aspect of your event deserves a written plan.

Some of the components of that plan may include:

Making every effort to get previous guests to attend —
- Offer special perks to anyone who attended last year's event — special seating or parking or an opportunity to attend a preview of the event.
- Get last year's attendees signed up before anyone else

(e.g. early bird invitation).

Pursuing specific strategies aimed at attracting new attendees —
- Get previous years' attendees involved in inviting friends and associates to this year's event.
- Add new features to your event that may attract those who had no previous interest (e.g. special entertainment, a celebrity, a one-of-a-kind auction item).

Set an attendance goal for your next event and back up the increase with specific strategies aimed at meeting that goal.

Aim for High Attendance

If the success of your library's fundraising event depends, for the most part, on a minimum number of paying guests, you will want to do whatever is possible to maximize attendance.

Follow these steps to help ensure you reach those attendance numbers:

1. **Build event ownership among as many people as possible early on in the process.** "If they own it, they will come." Get people personally connected to the event's success and not only will they attend, they will help get others there, too. That's why the most successful events

have several types of committees with large numbers of volunteers involved.
2. **Appoint a committee to sell tickets and get people to attend.** Be sure they know and accept that expectation before they agree to help. Offer inexpensive incentives for selling a set number of tickets.
3. **Make it attractive to buy multiple tickets.** Some events that include a meal, for instance, offer guests the opportunity to purchase an entire table of eight or 10. A golfing event might promote funding a foursome of golfers in addition to the individual option.

Steps Boost Ticket Sales

The financial success of a special event is often based on ticket sales. That's why it's so important that everyone involved takes responsibility for getting tickets sold. This is especially true if you are relying on volunteers for significant ticket sales.

To boost ticket sale success — and ultimately the success of your event overall:

- Plan backwards: The amount of revenue you want to generate will dictate both number of tickets you need to sell and ticket price. From there you can determine number of ticket sellers needed and minimum number of tickets each volunteer will need to sell.
- Get everyone involved in planning the event — not just those on the ticket committee — to agree to a minimum number of ticket sales.
- Agree that if volunteers cannot sell the agreed-to minimum ticket number, they will be responsible for buying the tickets they hold. (If you're confident this

measure will pass, take a vote on it to make it more official.)
- Use the pyramid method of selling: A certain number of captains are responsible, in turn, for enlisting a minimum number of ticket sellers.
- Make it appealing for attendees to purchase a group of tickets (e.g., table of eight). Provide corresponding benefits for those who purchase a group/table of tickets — preferred seating, special favors, recognition, etc.
- Use friendly competition to encourage ticket sales. Offer an incentive, for instance, to any who sells a certain number of tickets by a particular date.
- For an annual event, allow veteran volunteers the privilege of selling tickets to those who have purchased from them in previous years.
- Provide event sponsors with a limited number of tickets for their employees as a perk.

Tips for Getting Tickets Sold

To encourage all event planners to sell advance tickets to your next library event, offer a motivational incentive — a priceless item — based on meeting an established quota and deadline.

Such items might include:

1. Special parking privileges for a set period of time.
2. An invitation to an exclusive get-together — perhaps a pre-reception with your event's celebrity.
3. Special seating.
4. Recognition during the event — special name badges, standing to be recognized.
5. Not having to assist with some element of the event (e.g., cleanup).
6. A celebrity-autographed item.
7. Special membership privileges enjoyed by others who give at higher levels.

Additional Ticket Selling Tip

Buy inexpensive buttons for volunteers, staff and others to wear, both on and off the job, that read: "Ask Me About Tickets to the XYZ Agency's Holiday Gala!"

Keep the persons stocked in tickets to sell to impulse buyers, co-workers and other persons they encounter.

Encourage Event Buy-in to Boost Attendance

Want super attendance at your next event? Offer opportunities for the public to become involved without having to play a key role.

Here are a few examples of ways to involve the public and secure their attendance at your event:

- Create a contest to name the event. Publicize and reward the winner.
- Ask key persons to be present by virtue of their positions: elected officials, media representatives, local celebrities, etc.
- Name honorary guests or chairpersons or awards recipients who will want to enjoy the limelight of being present.
- Include a performance from youth that will bring their parents to the event.
- Host an exhibit of people's artwork, photographs or crafts to draw their presence.

Any and all linkages you can create between people and your event will enhance their desire to attend it.

Increase Event Attendance

Want more people to attend your events? Make children a part of your program. Parents never miss an opportunity to see their little ones take the limelight. If you involve children in some capacity, their parents are bound to attend your event.

Promote Notable Guests

If a notable person within your community RSVPs to your annual event invitation, why not use that as leverage to entice other prominent guests?

Acquiring a Who's Who guest list can help draw larger attendance at your primary events. Try the following tips to create a Who's Who event:

- Prior to sending out your mass invitation list, secure notables from your community to attend your event. Personally invite the mayor, area celebrities and prominent professionals to attend. When these notables agree to attend, ask to use their names to promote the event.
- Create a Notable Guests or Who's Who section on your mass invitations, e-invites, website and publicity materials that offers a list of prominent guests and a brief quote from each individual about your organization and why he or she wishes to attend.
- Create color-coded nametags for notable guests to wear at the event, so others may seek them out. (Get their approval before doing so).
- Ask a notable guest or two to speak on behalf of your organization the night of the event for an added special touch.

Fundraising for Libraries: How to Plan Profitable Special Events

Attendance-busting Ideas

To increase attendance for your event, come up with a way to get on the evening news the week of your event. To do that, come up with an attention-grabbing hook that local stations will want to carry.

Consider any of these ideas:

✓ Showcase a handful of loyal library patrons who will benefit from the funds being raised.

✓ If it's a themed event, enlist two or three people to be interviewed in costume.

✓ Share the name(s) of any celebrities who will be in attendance.

✓ Announce the chance for attendees to win a major prize.

Three Ways to Get Last Year's Attendees Back Again

It's been proven time and again: It's much easier to retain an existing customer or client than it is to recruit a new one. For that reason alone, it's important to retain your special event attendees from year to year, particularly if you want to grow attendance over time.

That being said, here are three ways to get last year's attendees back again:

1. **Evaluate their perceptions.** Don't hesitate to get attendees' opinions on what they liked and didn't like about your event. Survey them and/or talk to them within five days of the event, while everything is fresh in their minds. Pay as much attention to what guests enjoyed as you do their negative perceptions.

2. **Give past attendees first choice at subsequent years'** events. Send out your first round of invitations to last year's attendees, giving them top seating, best parking, first choice at seeing auction items and so forth. By distinguishing this loyal group from others, future first-time guests will also want to become part of this elite group.

3. **Recognize past attendees.** Include names of all ticket purchasers in your printed program. (You will, no doubt, need a cutoff date for printing purposes; however, this could even be a program insert prepared at the last minute.) Beside each name, include the number of years the individual has attended your special event. Also, you could ask all previous event attendees to stand and be recognized during the program.

Keep Your Event Vibrant, Attract New Guests

Though you are grateful for the loyal supporters who always attend your special events, attracting new people to your activities is the best way to continue to keep events vibrant. Here are some ideas to help you draw first-time visitors.

✓ **Build a theme around teams.** Best Friends or Co-workers are theme ideas that encourage existing supporters to bring a colleague or close friend to your event with them.

✓ **Keep up with chamber of commerce lists.** Look for newly established businesses in your community. Put them on your invitation list, and follow up with a phone call to the new entrepreneur to offer special pricing for all employees.

✓ **Build a Facebook event page.** Ask existing supporters with Facebook accounts to "like" your page, which shows their friends what is important to them. Include an RSVP link where their friends can see who else plans to attend. They may see that lots of their friends are going and decide to check it out.

✓ **Offer two-for-one event prices.** Your loyal supporters will be able to bring a friend for the same price as attending as a single — and you'll have a way to thank your longtime fans by allowing them to treat a friend to a fun venue.

✓ **Find a unique new venue.** If your family festival has always been held at City Park, look for an interesting alternative, like your local zoo, a botanical garden or art museum where there are new attractions and displays that people want to see anyway.

✓ **Feature well-known entertainment.** Featuring a favorite stand-up comic, acrobatic act, dance troupe, band or singer may be one of the easiest ways to bring new audiences to your event. Their fans may welcome the chance to attend the performance while supporting a worthy cause that is new to them.

Take Steps to Retain Past Years' Attendees

It's a proven fact that it's much easier to retain past event guests from year to year than to lure new guests to your annual event.

That being said, what specific strategies do you have in place to be sure past event attendees show up for this year's event? What reasons do you give your guests for wanting to remain loyal to your event? Don't just assume they will come; take proactive steps such as these:

- List attendees' names in each year's printed program along with the number of years they have attended.

- Invite veteran attendees to stand and be recognized at your event: "Will the following people, whose names I mention, please stand and be recognized for having attended our event for five or more years ..."

- Offer past attendees an early bird special of sorts if they purchase tickets in advance.

- Offer special perks (e.g., special seating, special name tags, a limited-edition print) to those who have attended for a minimum number of years.

- Allow previous years' attendees to keep the same table or seats if they choose.

Attendance-building Tips

There are any number of ways to optimize attendance for a special event. Here's one approach to consider:

- To reach out to the entire community or target certain neighborhoods, establish a promotions or marketing committee made up of one or more people representing various neighborhoods. Assign responsibility to each for getting the word out (or selling tickets) to all residents within his/her designated territory.

Library Event Profile

Authors Mingle With Guests at Library Fundraiser

Authors were on the move — literally — at the annual fundraiser for the Sacramento Public Library Foundation (Sacramento, CA).

During the seventh annual Authors on the Move gala, guests enjoyed a gourmet dinner and had an opportunity to visit with local and regional authors.

April Butcher, executive director, says the 40 participating authors moved table to table mingling with guests, rotating after spending 15 to 20 minutes at a table.

"The appeal of the event is definitely the authors," Butcher says. "Guests get to talk to the authors, and they have a good time doing it."

Participating authors also enjoyed the opportunity to promote and sell their books. Authors each had a table where guests could visit with them, purchase books and ask them to sign their books. Staff with the Borders bookstore chain coordinated the sale of the books.

The $200 tickets to the event included two keynote speakers (both authors), a raffle and live auction. Sponsorships ranged from $1,500 to $5,000.

Butcher offers advice for organizations interested in hosting a similar event:

- ✓ Be aware of what giving levels you are attracting. "Only do it if you want to build your donor base at the levels you expect people to give at to either buy the tickets or spend in the auction," she says.

- ✓ Secure volunteer support.

- ✓ Make the event fun and appealing to a broad audience. "Don't make decisions solely on your likes and dislikes," Butcher says. "Many people are vulnerable to decision making that way, but it is important to mix in all of the likes and dislikes both for buy-in and for a broader appeal."

Source: April Butcher, Executive Director, Sacramento Public Library Foundation, Sacramento, CA.
E-mail: abutcher@saclibrary.org

At a Glance —	
Event Type:	Gala
Gross:	$120,000
Costs:	$37,000
Net Income:	$83,000
Volunteers:	25
Planning:	400 to 500 hours
Attendees:	360
Revenue Sources:	Ticket sales, sponsorships, live auction, raffle and advertising
Unique Feature:	Authors visit with guests

Fundraising for Libraries: How to Plan Profitable Special Events.
Edited by Scott C. Stevenson.
© 2012 Stevenson, Inc. Published 2012 by Stevenson, Inc.

Fundraising for Libraries: How to Plan Profitable Special Events

Logistics: Food, Refreshments, Programs and More

Lights, camera, action! No one ever fully realizes all of the planning logistics that go on to make fundraising events for your library fun and winning experiences for those who attend. That's the way it's supposed to be. The time and attention you put into the details of your event setting the mood with lighting, decorations, food, refreshments, entertainment, your program and more — all impact the event's success and your guests' perceptions.

Seven Ambience-setting Steps

Creating event ambiance can be as simple as tweaking basic elements. To craft a memorable ambience, consider:

1. **Lighting.** When evaluating event venues, take a close look at the lighting. Avoid venues with fluorescent lighting that cannot be adjusted.

2. **Warmth.** Ask venue managers about the temperatures in the rental facility. Speak specifically about the number of guests attending the affair and how the temperature is controlled to ensure that guests are not chilled or melting at your event.

3. **Music.** Discuss acoustics with venue staff. Consider offering a string quartet at your event for calming musical backdrop, but ask if the acoustics at the venue will support this.

4. **Art.** To bring artistic flair to your event space, ask a local art gallery to offer pieces of art for auction that can be displayed throughout the venue.

5. **Tone.** Ask yourself: Does this venue set the right tone for the event? If looking for elegance, consider the look of the venue's ceiling, flooring, walls and window treatments.

6. **Color.** If your event calls for drama or elegance, evaluate event space based on the color scheme. When touring the space, consider if the color scheme offers the feel you desire. Steer clear of garish or outdated décor.

7. **Sparkle.** While you can easily add a touch of sparkle to table settings and decorations, determine if the venue offers this sparkle from the start. Chandeliers, candleholders or wall décor may provide the elegant touch you desire. If these items aren't present from the start, consider how to include this important aspect to the event.

Communicate With Florist to Maximize Value, Match Mood

While flowers may be seasonal, the impact they add to special events is timeless.

Flowers can also be one of the major overhead expenses. To maximize your investment in ambience and increase dollars that can benefit your programs:

✓ **Choose a florist appropriate to event size.** Your corner flower shop may be perfect for creating a floral spray for the head table at your employee tea, but you need more flower power for your annual gala's 50 centerpieces. Larger events require more staff, refrigeration, reliable delivery and setup of a sometimes-fragile product.

✓ **Plan floral arrangements well in advance.** A preflight consultation with your floral expert and flexibility in the final product can bring big savings. Decide which blossoms will be the best value at the time of your event, then talk spray treatments, trim and container colors to match your theme. A red palette with sprayed carnations may accomplish the same goal as more costly roses.

✓ **Negotiate little extras.** Ask the florist about an all-inclusive package where you agree to a set price for each centerpiece, topiary or swag, but get corsages or boutonnieres for honorees in the bargain. See if florists could waive rental or setup fees for non-floral items like trellises, urns and stands in exchange for posting a sign at the event that says, "Display Items courtesy of Downtown Florists."

✓ **Ask about repeat business discounts.** Review the past few years of flower purchases. Include those repeated annually in a contract bid for floral services for six months to a year. While you will pay extra for needs outside the contract, many shops will be eager to give you the best possible deal on other floral services, such as thank-you baskets for special supporters, when they know you are coming back.

✓ **Evaluate when a nursery can do double duty.** Can potted geraniums and dahlias destined for your facility's planters first be used as centerpieces for your spring luncheon? An accommodating nursery can wrap the pots in festive foil for your party before they are turned over to the groundskeeper.

Creative Mixers Boost Preprogram Activities

No matter how much effort you put into choosing the best speaker, menu and entertainment, pre-dinner activities may still be the bright spot for many who attend your special event. Be sure to invest planning time in this important event element.

To encourage mixing and conversation before people take their seats:

✓ **Plan a photo display.** Pictures are people magnets and conversation starters. Shots of donors/volunteers/supporters will have them looking for themselves and others in the crowd. Historical photos spark additional interest and "remember when" chats.

✓ **Bring in strolling entertainment.** Your local barbershop quartet or magician can engage and interact with guests — especially those who don't appear to be mixing with others.

✓ **Make a candid video of guests.** Ask persons what brought them to the event or why they support your cause. Even those who don't appear on camera will watch to see who is talking and where the camera goes next.

✓ **Offer refreshments throughout the crowd.** When serving staff walks around with appetizers, drinks or desserts, even those not mingling may enjoy refreshments.

✓ **Have games and prizes.** They don't have to be difficult or require skills, and the prizes need not be elaborate. A fishbowl with numbers to draw for pens, paperweights or other useful items with your organization's name on them will be enough to attract those who are looking for a diversion.

✓ **Host an information booth.** Ask personable volunteers to be on hand to visit with guests, give them brochures or tell them about volunteer opportunities within your library. An interactive kiosk with the same facts or a short digital presentation is another option.

Negotiate Speaker Deals

■ Don't sign a speaker's contract without negotiating first. Because of the economy, many speakers are quite willing to consider alternative offers: decreased speaking fees, travel expenses, additional services and more.

Lighting, Music, Nature Add Romance to Outdoor Event

Giving an outdoor event a romantic theme is one matter, but creating a truly romantic environment in an outdoor setting is more of a challenge. Once you resolve practical matters like pest control and location, consider these ideas to paint a romantic flair throughout your event:

❑ **Tents, canopies, pergolas and gazebos.** Hang a chandelier with battery-operated candles from the center, drape tables in unique fabrics and create an Arabian nights atmosphere filled with color and flattering light.

❑ **The peaceful sound of running water.** Check out your local garden center for lighted fountains of all shapes and sizes. Place them strategically for as many people as possible to enjoy them. Floating candles or flowers add even more romance. The store may loan them to you for free advertising.

❑ **Romantic — and wireless —music.** Portable wireless speakers can set different moods in different areas and allow more individualized volume control, so guests and couples can concentrate on each other.

❑ **Flowers that double as an additional fundraiser.** Order a supply of long-stemmed roses. Allow guests to purchase one (or more) for their dates. Include a ribboned card to tie to the rose, so it can be delivered to the table at the appropriate time.

❑ **Fragrance.** Your budget may not allow for real orchids, but you can infuse the area with the scent. More affordable blooms include lilacs and night-blooming jasmine.

❑ **Strolling violins and live piano.** "Of all the gin joints and towns in the world…" this piano player walked into your event and took requests for favorite romantic songs. A strolling violinist can fill in for variety, when the pianist is taking a break.

❑ **Dancing and romancing.** Book your town's best jazz trio or quartet that can nimbly shift from the bossa nova to a simple two-step. Variety inspires dancers with varying degrees of talent to get on the floor with the perfect excuse to get close to their date. Put your dance floor as close as possible to a moonlit pond or quiet courtyard.

Check New Master of Ceremonies's References

Be sure to check references as part of the selection process for a master of ceremonies. Here are some questions to ask those who have used a prospective emcee's services:

1. **How was the master of ceremonies perceived by the crowd?** Was he/she aloof or friendly? Did he/she use humor effectively and connect with the audience?

2. **Was he/she reliable?** Did he/she show up on time and deliver everything promised?

3. **Was he/she prepared?** Did the master of ceremonies have everything, including introductions, ready when he/she arrived?

4. **Did the individual appear poised in front of the audience?** Even though everyone gets at least somewhat nervous in front of a large group, did he/she effectively control his/her nervousness?

5. **Did the master of ceremonies convey a feeling of confidence to the audience?**

6. **Was he/she dressed properly?** Were there any personal traits that could be perceived as offensive to some?

7. **Could he/she adapt to changes?** If something went wrong at the last minute, did the individual respond properly? Could he/she ad-lib and fill in any surprise dead spots in the program or gracefully handle any other unexpected glitches?

Tips for Inexpensive Holiday Table Decorations

Decorating for your holiday event need not be a costly venture. Try these simple tips for decorating your holiday tables with less out-of-pocket spending:

✓ Buy live plants such as poinsettias to decorate your event, then reuse after the event to decorate your library or give as door prizes. Swirl pearls around the pot base.

✓ Fill inexpensive glass bowls or vases with pinecones from your nearest pine tree or with inexpensive holiday ball ornaments. Mix in red, green, silver or gold beads.

✓ Snip boughs from an evergreen and arrange them down the center of long tables. String among the boughs some white twinkle lights for a touch of class.

✓ Bake large gingerbread cookies and glaze for sheen. This decoration offers a great opportunity for volunteers to interact with staff to create a useful décor item. Store them for next year's event or hang on a tree after the event.

✓ Add tea lights on any table for an inexpensive yet elegant impact.

Match Keynote Speaker to Your Occasion

If you're planning an event complete with keynote speaker, select someone whose presence will complement the event's purpose and goals.

If you seek to draw attention to a matter of grave importance, that implies one kind of speaker. If you wish to use a speaker's celebrity status for drawing-card appeal, that narrows the focus of your selection.

To identify the best pool of speakers from which to choose, first ask yourself:

1. What should be the primary purpose of the keynote speaker at this event?

2. What will the audience expect — to be entertained? Enlightened? Inspired?

3. To what degree will this potential speaker impact attendance?

4. How have other audiences reacted to this speaker?

5. Will this speaker bring a certain degree of divisiveness — political or otherwise?

6. Is this speaker appropriate for the anticipated makeup of the audience?

7. To what other groups has this individual spoken in the past year?

8. Is the person reliable? Articulate? Dynamic? Knowledgeable on the intended subject?

9. Is there a cost to enlist this speaker? Is the fee within your budget?

10. What other services might the speaker provide — answer questions, visit with students/youth, sign his/her book, etc.?

As you narrow your choices in selecting the ideal person, be certain your top candidate is fully aware of your expectations, so there are no unanswered questions. In fact, put it all in writing.

Library Event Profile

Importance of Community Support When Planning Fundraisers

Held on May 12 in Hood River, Oregon, the Hood River County Library's annual Feast of Words fundraiser was a smashing success, netting almost $12,000 and attracting more than 100 people. The money is being used to support many essential services, such as magazine and newspaper subscriptions, a bilingual children's librarian and updated technology. As much as the community relies on a local library, libraries count on the community to pull off such successful events.

"The biggest reason our event was such a hit was our community is so supportive of our library," says Jen Bayer, president of the Hood River Library board of directors. "Also, the draw of doing something different helped bring people in."

The mouth-watering meals, desserts, wine and beer, all of which were donated by local businesses, helped to lure community members to the fundraiser. Silent and live auctions were also held to generate funds.

"Generous donations of food, beverages, the time it took to prepare the food and the items we auctioned off were essential to being able to pull this event off," adds Bayer. "We also had a few business sponsorships, which offset our out-of-pocket costs."

When it came to securing the community's support, Bayer and the board of directors relied in part on the local newspaper — several articles regarding the fundraiser were published in advance of the event. The team also distributed posters in businesses and utilized the Hood River Chamber of Commerce's web calendar, along with other regional electronic calendars, to spread the word.

In addition, foundation board members sent personal requests to individual potential donors and prepared a formal letter to request donations and business sponsorships. "That way, they had something to leave behind in case the person they needed to speak with wasn't available when they visited a business," Bayer said. Bayer even looked to the community when deciding on a date to hold the fundraiser. "Our biggest challenge was trying to schedule it around other community events — next year, we'll hold our event in late February or early March when there is less going on," she says.

Last but certainly not least, the board members relied on fundraiser volunteers to do most of the planning and implementation of the event. Bayer says the team is a "working board" with no paid staff, so all help is volunteer-based.

Source: Jen Bayer, Hood River County Library Foundation Board of Directors President. Hood River, OR. E-mail: info@hoodriverlibrary.org

Do Your Homework When Selecting Speakers

Coordinating a seminar that includes a featured speaker? Hosting an annual dinner that requires an after-dinner orator?

When it comes to selecting speakers, it's wise to do your homework. After all, just as a well-chosen speaker can make an event memorable for years to follow, a poor choice of speaker can ensure that few will attend your event a second time.

By following these guidelines, you can be more confident in the selection of an appropriate speaker for your next special event:

1. Understand the purpose/role of your speaker before selecting one.

2. Ask for a biography and list of previous topics covered.

3. Check references. Where has the individual appeared previously and what was the level of satisfaction?

4. Know that your speaker is fully aware of his/her role. Key him/her into the rest of what is to take place.

5. Ask for an advance copy or outline of the speech.

6. Agree on the amount of time to be allocated for speaking and whether follow-up questions will be invited.

7. Provide advance information to be confident that the speaker knows the anticipated makeup of the audience and is aware of any special needs or preferences.

8. Know in advance the method of delivery to be used. Will the remarks include an overhead, handouts, etc.?

9. Confirm everything in writing, and touch base within a day or two of the event to review final plans.

10. Review with the speaker remarks that will be used to introduce him/her to ensure accurateness and appropriateness.

Take the time early on in your event planning to make the right speaker choice. Your attention to the selection of a speaker and your conscientiousness in making your expectations crystal clear to the speaker will make for a more meaningful and memorable experience for everyone.

Tips for Choosing a Caterer

If your library's special event requires a caterer, consider the following when selecting the caterer who is perfect for your event:

- **Check local directories to find caterers or ask for referrals** from other nonprofits that have offered premium events with the help of caterers.

- **Interview at least three caterers** with pricing options and food selections from which to choose.

- **Ask each catering service for references from within the past year.** Call on each reference and ask about quality, pricing and professionalism of each caterer.

- **Ask to review the caterer's portfolio** that shows food presentation and pictures of finished catered events.

- **Schedule a tasting.** Ask that each caterer offer a broad sampling of what he/she can offer your event.

- **Discuss your budget and weigh pricing carefully.** By no means is the price a caterer quotes you initially the final price. Work together to find cost-cutting measures to maintain quality but reduce costs.

- **Get it in writing.** Once pricing and service options are selected, ask for a final contract with the caterer and review it well in advance of the event. Don't hesitate to ask questions and review the fine print to ensure you're not left with hidden costs.

Careful Planning Is First Step for Large-group Catering

You're anticipating a crowd of 500 or more for your next fundraiser, your menu is planned and the caterer is known for great food and service. You're done, right?

Not quite.

Take these steps to help avert most potential disasters and guarantee success:

✓ **Prepare for smooth traffic flow for buffets.** Offer several serving areas where guests can get salads, entrees, side dishes and dessert in one trip. Allow enough space so both sides of the serving table can be accessed. Catering staff can visit tables to offer beverage refills to avoid drink lines.

✓ **Consider special dietary needs of all guests.** Few things are more disappointing to attendees than buying a ticket for a catered event and finding there's little they can eat. Ask your caterer to focus on tasty dishes that are low in sodium, cholesterol and sugar. Offer a substantial side dish, like meatless pasta salad, that can double as a main course for vegetarians.

✓ **Check facility logistics.** Walk through the facility with your banquet manager to review electrical outlets, fire safety restrictions and proximity to emergency exits. Determine in advance where extra food can be stored at proper serving temperature and how serving vessels can be refilled.

✓ **Review your backup facility.** Be ready for rain, shine or power outages with a banquet layout for two facilities. If the venue must change at the last minute, have staff stationed at every entrance (including the parking lot) to direct guests to the new location.

✓ **Taste all menu items well in advance.** Even if you're familiar with the caterer and trust the product, ask for a preview for yourself and two or three others who have some knowledge of food and cooking. Is the chicken too spicy for some? Are the vegetables crisp and fresh? Be candid with your critiques and any changes you think are necessary, so adjustments can be made.

Five Dinner Logistics Ideas

Planning an event that includes a sit-down dinner? What can you do to add fun and intimacy to the experience?

As you plan the details of that event, consider these five possibilities:

1. Make your event more organic and less controlling by assigning tables rather than seats.

2. Invite members of each table to make a toast to one another at some point during the course of the dinner.

3. Leave a chair open at each table for the host(s) to visit with guests. (This works best for smaller events.)

4. Place a sticker underneath one chair at each table. At the dinner's conclusion, invite each person to check his/her chairs. The person with the sticker underneath his/her chair gets to take home that table's centerpiece.

5. Have guests move to different tables for dessert and coffee to encourage mixing groups.

Fundraising for Libraries: How to Plan Profitable Special Events

Promoting and Publicizing Your Event

What you do, the steps you take to get the word out prior to, during and immediately following your special event will all impact its success. Many special events fail to accomplish nearly what they could have accomplished due to lack of advance promotion. This represents a great time to grab the public's attention for your library, to make them aware of your programs and to build attendance for your money-making event.

Make the Most of a Volunteer Publicity Committee

As you evaluate the publicity needs for your library's special event, evaluate your volunteer corps as well. Do you have volunteers whose background or talents are a good match for a specific type of publicity?

Even in large organizations, it's most effective to think small when recruiting volunteers to serve on your publicity committee. One well-rounded and experienced individual, accompanied by an assistant chairperson, may be more than adequate for some events.

If your major event or slate of several upcoming events will require more extensive publicity efforts, think first of the categories of coverage including:

- **Written copy.** Public service announcements, press releases and photographs are among the most useful vehicles for informing the community of your events. A person who writes news releases well and who can draft copy for radio, television and newspaper announcements will be a valuable addition to your committee. Even if the volunteer has never had professional experience in these areas, possessing the skill to write concise facts for editors and producers to use will be appreciated.

- **Personal contact.** Every organization has an individual who has friends and contacts to enlist to help your cause. This person may have excellent telephone skills and be diligent about follow-up calls to media or sponsors who have agreed to help you with publicity. A community liaison with broad-based knowledge of publicity resources should be the primary contact for media, which helps avoid the number of duplicate calls received by others on the committee.

- **Attractive presentations.** Once you have found individuals who can communicate well both on paper and in person, a designer, decorator or artistic person can round out the group. The combination of well-written facts, attractive graphics for printed materials or promotional posters, and a pleasant individual to present them to media representatives will help your organization stand above those who simply call or mail news releases.

Coordinating Internal and External Publicity

Go beyond matching volunteers to publicity tasks, as detailed above, to make sure your employees know details of special events as well.

When paid staff produce newsletters and brochures for activities, involve them in the volunteer efforts to increase the impact of your combined efforts.

Paid staff and volunteers both bring expertise to the table, and a volunteer may have a more flexible schedule to meet with media at the media's convenience. By the same token, one of your paid staff may have professional media contacts who would be willing to work with your organization's volunteer.

Look at all resources within your organization, whether they are offered by volunteers or staff. Pair them when the combination of skills and chemistry is logical to save time and increase creative energy.

Have a clear description of duties for each member of the publicity committee, so each member knows what he/she should pursue, and what his/her fellow committee members are doing. Should they decide between themselves that one is better suited than another for a specific duty, allow them the flexibility they need to achieve the publicity objective as long as everyone is agreeable.

Structure and clear job descriptions are important guides for volunteers, but good chemistry and common interest in obtaining the best possible coverage for your event are the best qualifications for volunteers on the publicity committee.

Your involvement is important to them as a resource and a guide, but if you have asked the best-qualified persons to serve, all you will really need are regular updates on their progress, and to be sure they have support they need from other volunteers and staff.

Fundraising for Libraries: How to Plan Profitable Special Events

Create Event Flyers That Pop

Producing eye-catching event flyers is still one of the most cost-effective ways to advertise your event. Flyers need not be complicated; a few unique aspects can have your flyer drawing lots of attention. Try these tips when creating your next event flyer:

❑ Create a flyer unique in size and shape. Cut flyers into shapes such as stars for a dramatic impact. Go with a larger-than-standard size, thinking beyond 8 1/2 x 11 inches.

❑ Get your complete message on the flyer, but allow for white space, which lets the reader absorb the information with ease without feeling inundated with details.

❑ Use clean, easy-to-read fonts in a large point size for easy readability.

❑ Don't forget the details. Include the who, what, when, where, why and how of your event.

❑ Align flyer images, shape and style with other print advertising to develop a common theme and recognition for your events.

❑ Post flyers throughout your region the week prior to an event. This effort, along with other publicity, creates a double dose of advertising sure to draw guests.

Carefully Review Your Event's Press Release

Getting pre-event publicity for your special event is vital to its success. You can have the greatest event ever planned and hundreds of dedicated volunteers lined up to make it happen, but it's doomed to failure if no one knows about it.

Press releases represent one of many ways to get the word out on upcoming events.

Before sending out a press release announcing your event, read it over as if seeing it for the first time. Is it understandable? Does it answer all the questions as to who, what, where, why, when and how?

If possible, have someone who doesn't know about your group or event read the press release, looking specifically to determine if it is informative and all contact information is there.

Here is a sample press release that illustrates how to cover some of the basics:

Your Organization
111 Main Street
Hometown, USA

For More Information Contact
Ima Knowitall, Public Relations Director
Phone (555) 555-5555 or E-mail ima@yourorganization.com

Nov. 1, 2012

For immediate release

Your Organization's Annual Dinner Slated for Nov. 22

HOMETOWN, State — Your Organization, 987 Blank St., will hold its annual dinner Sunday, Nov. 25, 2012 at the Old Inn, 123 Elm St. Social hour will start at 6:30 p.m. with dinner following.

Guest speaker will be John Smith noted author and lecturer. Smith will speak about "How Widgets Have Changed the World."

Smith received his doctorate on widgets from Hardknocks University in 1991 and has written 10 books on the subject. His latest book, "How Widgets Have Changed the World," has been on the best seller list since being published. Autographed copies will be available to purchase following the program.

Tickets are available to the public and are $20 per person. Reservations must be made by 5 p.m. Monday, Nov. 19 by calling (555) 555-5555.

Develop a Press Release Style Sheet

Do you use formal titles of Mr. and Mrs.? Do you refer to your organization by an acronym or nickname? Do you share your mission statement in the lead or last sentence?

These are just some of the many questions that come up when writing a press release for your organization. Get past the questions and instead spend your time focusing on the meat of the article by having a style sheet on hand that addresses how to properly format key information in press releases and other written correspondence to the news media.

A style sheet will help answer the above questions, as well as:
• What's the correct tag line to describe the organization?

• Must board member names be included in every release?
• What phone number and e-mail contact should be listed for more information?
• What's the proper wording for directions to our event?
• Who is the designated press contact?
• What acronyms need to be explained?

One final benefit? A style sheet helps guarantee a consistent message, no matter who writes the news release or publicity materials.

Well-crafted Press Releases Maximize Pre-event Publicity

Is getting the word out about your library's special event one of the most important aspects of the planning process? The most cost-efficient way to publicize your event is with a press release to the local media. But while you're sending in your finely crafted press release, so are many other nonprofits.

How do you make your release stand out from all the others to help guarantee it gets published on time and catches the attention of a reporter or assignment editor for a feature story? Here are tips to make sure your press release — and your event — both get the attention they deserve:

✓ **Use a style guide.** Some publications use an in-house style guide, but most follow basic rules set forth in guide books such as "The Associated Press Stylebook." If your release is written in the same style as the publication, busy journalists rushing to meet a deadline will not have to rewrite it.

✓ **Write the release to match the purpose.** For the community calendar portion of the newspaper, write in the style of the calendar listing, not a full release. Include only necessary facts. A notice sent to a radio or TV station to be read as a public service announcement (PSA) should also be an abbreviated version of the full release.

✓ **Develop a style sheet of your own.** It will give each press release a consistent feel and flair, regardless of who writes it.

Get the Word Out

- Looking for ways to promote your next event? Produce business card-sized announcements that volunteers and staff can hand out to those with whom they come in contact. Include the name of the event, the date/time, contact information and a website where recipients can go to get more information.

Radio Helps the Public Tune Into Your Events

Enlisting local radio stations' support can increase community awareness of your event while attracting new donors.

Many stations support charitable causes via public service announcements (PSAs), sponsorships and radio personalities appearing and broadcasting live from fundraisers.

Begin engaging radio stations in your cause by first identifying which station's music or broadcast format is best suited to your target audience.

Research by the Arbitron Company identifies what age groups and genders listen to which stations and when. This information can help nonprofits determine how much air time to buy, and what time of day to air ads to reach a desired demographic.

Once you know which stations to target, approach station managers and news personnel as you would major sponsors. Offering to pay for some commercials during peak rate time may result in additional free time in slower programming hours.

The proposal you present to radio station management may include:

- **Brief appearances by you or event chairs.** Ask to be a guest on an on-air talk or news show to spend a few minutes telling listeners about your event and its purpose. Include information and phone numbers for tickets and times. Some radio stations will agree to be a ticket outlet as well.

- **Celebrity appearances.** Most radio stations send on-air personalities to an event site to do brief updates about the success of the event, and encourage others to join the festivities.

- **Public service announcements.** These are like free commercials for your cause. Free airtime may be at a premium since many organizations make such requests, but do ask.

- **Event sponsorship.** Such a request usually requires many months of planning, as many radio stations are committed far in advance. Think of ways the station will benefit from an association with your organization, offering major recognition status in any publicity you receive from other media as well. But remember that competing stations will not be likely to offer their support at the same time.

Spark Interest in Attractions With Past Event Photos

Your winter gala was the talk of the town last year with spectacular food, decorations and entertainment — and you have the photos to prove it.

Why not use some of the best photos to promote or generate interest in your upcoming party?

Here are some creative ways in which to incorporate those photographs:

- **Save the date postcard.** Use one terrific, colorful photo or a sampling of fun pictures on the front of your save-the-date card with the message, "Don't miss the fun this year!"

- **Use them as background on print ads.** A panoramic shot of your event venue filled with happy crowds and festive decorations from last year can give potential guests a great visual image of themselves attending this year's party and send the message, "This is the place to be on February 22nd."

- **Make a large photo puzzle.** Choose your best crowd shot and create a gigantic puzzle to be cut into a reasonable number of pieces (250, 500). Include them as

teasers in your invitations, asking guests to bring their unique piece to the event to build the complete puzzle.

- **Hold an online caption contest.** It's not unusual to post event photos on your website, but asking for amusing caption contributions for some of the most entertaining can add fun while promoting the next occasion. Offer prizes in various categories the night of the event.

- **Set up a slide show** in your library's lobby a few weeks ahead of time. Interested visitors can enjoy the show, pick up ticket information, make reservations, volunteer for a committee or even make a donation at the same time.

- **Make a Facebook album and event page.** Facebook has become one of the most affordable and efficient vehicles for publicizing special events. You can combine a large photo album with the RSVP interface to get a reasonable idea of potential attendance. Even those who don't attend may enjoy seeing pictures of their friends and will learn more about your cause.

Capture Event's Essence For Publicity Photographs

Photographs are worth a 1,000 words, or so it is said, so why not make the most of your publicity photos? Follow these savvy tips for acquiring publicity photos to promote your special events and your nonprofit in general:

- Capture interior and exterior shots of your library for use on your website and to supply to the media for stories about your programs. Be sure to catch people and patrons in action for these shots to give the photo a lively touch.

- Capture photos to submit with your press releases. A newspaper is more likely to run your story if you have captivating photos to go along with it.

- Obtain an architect's rendering of your building updates or additions to include with stories about your library and its expansion.

- Create images in digital form for ready use by the media. Post a media tab at your website where media professionals can easily access the photos for news purposes.

- If you're sponsoring an annual event, arm your staff and board members with cameras to snap candid photos to use for publicity purposes. The more choices available, the better. People love seeing themselves, and candid shots create a lively portrait of the excitement of your events.

Promote Your Event Online

As nonprofits continue to expand their reach through online resources, it makes sense that websites that help promote events would create opportunities for nonprofits to access their services.

Here is what you need to know about these three major event-promotion websites:

- Eventbrite lets nonprofits create a customizable event page, spread the word through social media, collect money and gain visibility. Events that are free to attend are listed at no charge. Events that charge entrance fees can be listed for a fee (2.5 percent plus $0.99 per ticket or payment processing using credit cards, PayPal, or Google Checkout for no more than 3 percent of ticket price). Eventbrite also offers Eventbrite for Causes, a special component of services and resources just for nonprofits.

- Eventful offers a free component and paid upgrade. The free component lets organizations post events and add venues to the website. Upgrading allows promotion through its weekly events guide e-newsletter.

- Zvents, according to its website, lets people "discover and choose fun things to do." Basic listings are free, with premium listings that include images, videos and links to tickets starting at $19.95.

Retail Stores May Be Partners in Publicizing Your Event

Retail stores in your community often seek ways to support local organizations with donations, gift cards and percentages of sales to benefit a cause. They also may consider one of the following proposals to help you publicize your event to increase attendance.

Provide staff with colorful tees or apparel. The checker at the grocery store, the teller at the bank and the waiter at the family diner can wear your event attire while on the job and engage customers in conversation about specifics.

Ask for space on their marquees. Banks, drug stores and malls are a few businesses that often have electronic billboards where specials are displayed. See if they will put the five Ws of your gala in the lineup — especially if they are located at a busy intersection where drivers wait in traffic.

Sell event tickets. With cashiers already in place, some businesses may agree to be a point of purchase for event tickets like benefit concerts, fireworks displays and other activities where reservations are not needed. Make it easy and feasible for employees to integrate into their usual duties.

Promote you in social media. Businesses have Facebook pages and websites that their customers follow for news of sales and specials. Ask them to publicize your event on their pages, explaining why they choose to be involved with your organization, and encouraging others to support you.

Use your name in advertising. Ask them to add a line to radio or television spots or in print ads such as, "Proud supporter of Memorial Library's Family Day on May 12." The relationship with your institution helps them build their reputation as a community booster.

Give a friends and family ticket discount. By offering special event pricing to a large group of employees, you also gain built-in publicity as they buy their own tickets, then offer them to others they know at a better price than they could get by calling your office directly.

Library Event Profile

Promote Your Library's Value With Fun Quiz

If you're looking for a way to let the community know how vital your services are, why not take a page from the Ferguson Library (Stamford, CT)? At their recent Eat, Play, Read fundraising event guests could learn about some of the library's impressive statistics by viewing signs placed strategically around the building. They also were able to take a Ferguson Fun Facts quiz while touring the renovated space.

Communications Supervisor Linda Avellar says it was a good way to introduce guests, who might not have set foot in the library in a while, to all that the library does and how important library services are in tough economic times.

Source: Linda Avellar, Communications Supervisor, the Ferguson Library, Stamford, CT. E-mail: linda@fergusonlibrary.org

Shown at right is a portion of the fun facts quiz Ferguson Library used during the Eat, Play, Read fundraising event. Use this to get ideas for your organization's own fun facts quiz.

Content not available in this edition

Fundraising for Libraries: How to Plan Profitable Special Events.
Edited by Scott C. Stevenson.
© 2012 Stevenson, Inc. Published 2012 by Stevenson, Inc.

Fundraising for Libraries: How to Plan Profitable Special Events

Why not set a goal of making your library's special event one of the most memorable, one of the most Wow-factor events in your community and surrounding area? Doing so will ensure that it becomes a highly-attended annual event in subsequent years. In fact, that Wow-factor may require that you limit attendance as time goes on. What a problem that would be!

Jazz Up Your Event

Every event needs that Wow factor. Here are a dozen inexpensive ways to create a fresh, crowd-pleasing event:

1. Pick a theme that reinforces your message and gives you something visual to work with in all planning areas. Use the theme colors and style consistently on all print and graphic pieces: logo, signage, linens, backdrop, tables, etc.

2. Recruit local experts, newscasters, authorities or celebrities as emcees, keynote speakers or hosts. These personalities add flair as accomplished speakers who exude enthusiasm.

3. Use large props or backdrops from theater companies or schools to add some visual interest.

4. Try interactive centerpieces like puzzles or toys. Be careful not to distract the audience from the program if a keynote speaker is planned.

5. Build in surprises. A surprise appearance builds excitement.

6. Turn an ordinary dinner event into a cooking class where guests cook, serve and ultimately eat the meal.

7. Pre-draw a mural pertaining to the event and invite attendees to paint it. Give the finished piece to the guest of honor.

8. Print trivia pertaining to your organization or cause on cocktail napkins to use as icebreakers.

9. Offer dance lessons as part of the cocktail hour.

10. Hire local artists to create centerpieces to be auctioned off at the event's end.

11. Don't be afraid to experiment and take calculated risks to improve an event.

12. Within two weeks of your event's conclusion, bring key people together to brainstorm what worked, and what didn't work, and start planning how you will wow next year's crowd.

Surprise Elements Keep Audiences Intrigued, Delighted

People look forward to your library's parties not only because they support a worthy cause, but because they are festive and entertaining. You want to keep attendees coming back with fresh activities and features. Here are some tips for serving up an element of surprise:

✓ **Transform an ordinary facility.** Incorporating elements like dramatic tension structures and lighting can turn a gymnasium into a movie set.

✓ **Invite an unexpected VIP guest.** Does a nationally known figure or entertainer have ties to your community? Whom do your contacts know who might enjoy coming to your event if they won't be dogged by the media?

✓ **Feature artistic food.** Delight guests with ornate edible centerpieces, fruit bouquets, dessert towers and ice sculptures. It's even better if you can have the prep artist on hand for garnishing demonstrations.

✓ **Give generous prizes to random guests.** It's popular to offer floral centerpieces to the person at the table whose birthday is closest to the event date to take home. Stick a

$100 gift card to a local retailer on the bottom.

✓ **Present an unexpected major award.** You'll want to ensure in advance that the recipient will attend, then honor them with a musical and video tribute prepared by a top-secret committee.

✓ **Hire surprise entertainment.** Your audience expects your local jazz quintet, but imagine their delight if a world-famous band shows up on stage making a spectacular musical entrance after the opening act.

✓ **Light up the sky.** Announce that there will be a special event at the end of the evening. Then begin a spectacular fireworks display with a theme that has special meaning for your organization.

✓ **Save a pivotal announcement for the occasion.** You have reached a fundraising goal that allows you to break ground on your library addition. You have made an important alliance that will allow you to reach national or worldwide audiences. Share the good news with your most loyal supporters in a festive environment first.

Give Your Events Attention-getting Invitations

Planning time is drawing near for your next event, and the occasion calls for a creative, memorable invitation. Where do you start?

First, consider the number of people on the guest list. The smaller the number, the more creative you can be. Next, determine how you will distribute the invitations. Will they be mailed or delivered by some other method?

Now, take a mental inventory of the talents of your staff, volunteers and patrons. Do you have people who love to paint, decorate, perform, sing or arrange flowers?

Now that you're thinking beyond traditional paper and envelopes, you may dream up some exceptional ideas — such as these — for inviting guests to your next event:

✓ **Say it with flowers.** Check prices and options with a local florist. Choose a pretty and affordable arrangement of seasonal flowers or something as simple as a single daisy and sprig of greenery with ribbon or colorful tissue, depending on your budget and guest list. Provide preprinted RSVPs with the bouquet.

✓ **Use recyclable materials.** Use paint markers to write event specifics on the outside of glass jars, then fill with candies, spices, flavored coffee beans or potpourri.

✓ **Send a message in a bottle.** Buy a quantity of discount-priced bottles with corks (often available for a dollar or two). Roll your one-sheet invitation into a scroll and tie tightly so it's easy to get out of the bottle. The delighted recipients can read your event specifics when they unroll the scroll (use colorful paper and whimsical fonts). Write the person's name and/or address on the bottle and use stickers or curling ribbon around the neck so they know at a glance it contains something special.

✓ **Wow them with a singing telegram.** Gather some of your talented volunteer performers to deliver a singing or dancing invitation. They can hand the information and response cards to the invited guest. Add to the fun by having your performers dress in full costume and arrive in a vehicle decorated in a way that clearly identifies your organization to reduce the possibility of surprises. Send teaser cards a week or two before to alert people that a "live" invitation will arrive soon.

✓ **Look for unusual, mailable containers.** Small round tubes in glossy colors or shiny square boxes that look like wrapped packages can often be mailed, depending upon size and shape. Design mock-ups of a special package you hope to mail, including ribbons, stickers, stamps or decorations you intend to use, and take it to the post office to see if it complies with mailing requirements and what it would cost to mail. Make suggested modifications and check again. Once you have approval, gather volunteers and give detailed instructions to ensure uniform assembly.

✓ **Engage a team of persons to deliver invitations.** If you plan to hand-deliver invitations, check with local delivery services or arrange volunteers to deliver batches of special invitations in or near their own neighborhoods. Remember that invitations don't always have to be mailed in envelopes, but be sure printed materials with time, place, costs and response cards are included for the recipients' convenience.

Library Event Profile

Big Trucks Provide Big Way For Families to Support Library

Every two years, supporters of the Madison Public Library (Madison, NJ) enjoy supporting the library through a creative event with a true, keep-on-trucking theme.

Started in 2008, the Touch a Truck benefit is a community event in which owners of trucks bring the vehicles for children and grown-ups alike to touch, climb inside, and take photos by.

Pat Tagg, Friends of the Madison Public Library chair, says they partnered with the Rotary Club of Madison and the Madison YMCA for the event. This year's event drew more than 1,000 parents and children and raised more than $4,500 in ticket sales alone.

The event featured three dozen vehicles, including two moving vans, a mini excavator, and a Ghostbusters Mobile. The Saint Barnabas Fire Safety House and TUMBLEBUS, a school bus retrofitted with jungle gym equipment, were among the most popular vehicles. Romanelli's and Whole Foods sold food and refreshments and Friends of the Madison Public Library ran a face painting and tattoo tent.

"Generally the funds are given over to the library to use where needed," Tagg says.

Tagg says they learned from the event's first year how to make the following years' fundraisers more successful. "Having one event behind us to learn from, gaining sponsorships and having an effective and organized board, plus an attractive and exciting program for kids and their families all influence the event's success."

Revenue sources include sponsorships through various local businesses and area residents. Contributors include Andy Breckman, creator of the USA Network's series "Monk," and his wife, Beth Landau.

"The generosity of our sponsors, the largest ones being anonymous, has been outstanding," she says. "Plus, the library board of trustees was extremely generous."

Also helping build on success in the event's second year, she says, was the addition of live music by a local student band, The Spazz, specialty vehicles and an extended gift auction.

Source: Pat Tagg, FMPL Chair, Madison Public Library, Madison, NJ.

Preview/Patron Party Ideas Extend Event's Excitement

Pre-event or patron parties provide festive opportunities for you to thank your major donors, committee volunteers and chairs for their diligent work, as well as to extend the celebration.

Consider these ideas to thank key people involved with your event:

❑ **Progressive dinner.** Ask three supporters with large homes, beautiful gardens or spectacular patios to host either hors d'oeuvres, the main course or a dessert buffet.

❑ **VIP treatment.** Treat patrons to a VIP party complete with swag bags filled with fragrance samples, small boxes of fine chocolates and other delicacies. Give them mingling time with event celebrities or keynote speakers, and gold or silver wristbands or ribbons designating VIP status. Make a video while interviewing them about why they support your cause and screen it during the main event.

❑ **Golf and spa outing.** Make a whole day and night of it by offering a golf or spa party to couples or individuals the day of your evening event. Arrange for manicure, pedicure, facial or massage services at a country club where those who prefer golf can hit the links instead. They'll be relaxed and ready for the evening's festivities.

❑ **Private auction.** Save your top 10 choice auction items for a private sale at the pre-event party. Opportunities to bid on automobiles, vacation packages, exquisite jewelry or original artwork may increase event ticket sales from serious supporters and bidders.

❑ **Stay-at-home party.** Several days before the big event, deliver baskets with a bottle of wine, gourmet cheeses and meats, baked goods, fresh fruit and pastries to patron donors at their homes or offices, along with valet parking passes, seating assignments and programs for the day of the event.

Five Interactive Ways to Get Your Guests Involved

No matter what type of event you're having, guests are likely to stay longer and be more interested in attending again the following year if they are having a great time. The more interested they are, the more likely they are to learn more about your library's mission and become involved. Here are some great activities to add to your next event to get your guests involved and, in some cases, raise additional funds:

1. **Red-carpet entrance** — Give your guests the royal treatment when they arrive with a red-carpet entrance.

2. **Ballroom dancing** — Invite instructors from a local college or studio to come and give a brief ballroom dancing presentation, followed by a bit of instruction for those interested.

3. **Dunking booth** — Is there a fun-loving volunteer or board member who would be willing to get wet for your cause, or even a local celebrity whom people love to

hate? Invite him or her to come and sit in the dunking booth and take potshots from your guests.

4. **You be the judge** — Have two local chefs cook their signature dishes and let guests vote on their favorite. Or let guests sample local wines or craft brews and decide on the winner. On a small scale, these can easily fit into a larger event and generate additional interest.

5. **Strike a pose** — There are a multitude of ways you can involve your guests using photography. Stage paparazzi to work your red-carpet entrance and click candids of your guests arriving, or rent a photo booth where guests can emerge with a silly string of four poses.

For kid-friendly events, think hands-on stations. Kids love getting messy, and love take-aways even more. Crafts, cooking or science, depending on the nature of your event and mission, are all great places to start.

Draw Interest With a Spin-to-win Wheel

There are many ways to attract event participants to an informational/sign-up booth, but few are more effective than a free-standing spin wheel. Though such wheels are simple and well-known, guests will almost invariably line up for the chance to participate, not because of the prizes offered, which can be quite small — pens, small snacks, key chains, etc. — but simply for the thrill of spinning the wheel. And if you feel you need a little more draw, you can easily have one section

of the wheel offer participants the chance to enter a drawing for a larger grand prize, which should be displayed on-site, if possible.

Prize wheels can be purchased online, but they can also be constructed from scratch — not a small project, but doable for a skilled volunteer or supporter. A good wheel can be used for years, and once a crowd has gathered, conversations about your mission, cause or project follow naturally.

Library Event Profile

Opus and Olives Showcases Best-Selling Authors

Seven is a lucky number for organizers of Opus & Olives, a special event that benefits The Friends of the Saint Paul Public Library (Saint Paul, MN).

Organizers of the event, which celebrated its seven-year anniversary in 2010, say community participation has doubled since its inception in 2004. The 2010 event, held at the Crowne Plaza Riverfront Hotel Saint Paul (Saint Paul, MN), attracted 800 guests and netted $105,000.

Wendy Moylan, the library's director of institutional relations, says the event was inspired by a similar event in Houston, TX.

"We started by seeking co-hosts Pioneer Press/Twin Cities.com," Moylan says. "We were looking for an opportunity to raise awareness of The Friends to new people. We worked with an advisory committee and a board member's design firm in the beginning to develop an event brand that would be unique and have deliberately stuck with it."

Moylan says the event attracts attention because of the opportunity for attendees to spend time with some of America's top authors. The 2010 event featured authors Stanley Trollip, Adriana Trigiani, Joshilyn Jackson, Dave Kindred and Roy Blount Jr.

In addition, Delta Air Lines, an event sponsor, donated to a raffle two round-trip business-class tickets to Europe, Africa or the Middle East, which drew the attention of 300 people, each of whom paid $100 each for a raffle ticket.

The base ticket price for the event was $125. Tables at the event were available at the $1,250, $2,500 and $3,500 levels. Corporate tables started at $2,500. Sponsorships were also available at $5,000, $10,000, $20,000 and $30,000.

Moylan says as guests arrived, they picked up nametags with table assignments. As they approached the reception area, they received a book bag with an event logo.

The authors, whose books were available for purchase at the event, were present as guest speakers and available to sign books and chat before and after dinner.

Moylan credits volunteers for the success of the event.

"Volunteers have been key to defining the scope of the program for each event, as well as the event as a whole," she says. "They recommend authors based on presentation skills and perceived appeal to the audience. At the event, they are critical in making people feel welcomed and thanked."

Tremendous support for the event also came from sponsors. Depending upon sponsorship levels, sponsors received exclusive ads and their name and logo on all newspaper ads, print materials and electronic communications, the opportunity to speak from a podium, receive a private reception with the authors and have multiple tables of guests with the author(s) sitting with their guests at dinner.

Moylan says for future events, she would limit the time speakers are allowed to talk.

"Each year we struggle with trying to control our speakers," she says. "On average, one each year will talk too long, which disrupts the flow and spirit of the event. We will look at means to cut a speaker off without being disrespectful, because our responsibility is to our guests."

But despite the occasional verbosity of a speaker, Moylan says overall the event was an achievement.

"The venue was filled to capacity, people consistently say they love this event and profits continue to increase," she says. "Year after year, we find that our friends bring their friends, who then become our friends. So while event profits increase, we also have attracted new board members, as well as individual and corporate gifts due to connections made at the event."

Source: Wendy Moylan, Director of Institutional Relations, The Friends of the Saint Paul Public Library, Saint Paul, MN.

At a Glance —

Event Type:	Dinner with multiple speakers
Gross:	$205,000
Costs:	$100,000
Net Income:	$105,000
Volunteers:	20
Planning:	10 months
Attendees:	800
Revenue Sources:	Ticket sales, raffle, corporate sponsorship, book sales
Unique Feature:	Nationally known authors visit with guests and speak at event

Involve More Guests With Entertaining Activities

Raising funds for and increasing awareness of your mission may be the purpose of your event, but many who attend will see it as an opportunity to have fun and socialize.

Here are some tips you can use to help increase audience involvement and entertainment:

- **Create a central attraction in the middle of the room,** like a large cupcake display or dance floor so everyone feels involved regardless of seating assignment.

- **Brief your entertainment on the people in the audience,** including amusing stories the entertainers can bring up in their routines.

- **Adapt an audience participation game** like "Let's Make a Deal" or "The Price Is Right" to your program where any guest has a chance to be on stage or win a prize.

- **Offer a scavenger hunt.** Compile a list of common items (shoelace, nail clipper, pocketknife, flashlight) that guests might not normally carry to a party. Ask those who have the item to share why they brought them.

- **Try "Name That Tune"!** Everyone has a party horn. Play snippets of music to see who can identify it first by blowing his/her horn. Let the top players compete for a grand prize.

- **Feature some popular casino games.** Have a few that require skill, like blackjack, and others like roulette or dice that anyone can play.

- **Hire a cartoonist.** A quick sketch artist can float between tables drawing guests, and then make a display at the end of the evening for all to view.

- **Suggest a table switch.** Put five or six different colors of decoration on individual desserts. Ask each person to have the last course with someone else who has a green flower, an orange star or a purple crown.

Library Event Profile

Host a Murder Mystery Night

It doesn't take a detective to figure out that a murder mystery night can be an entertaining and engaging fundraiser that will attract crowds and raise profits and awareness for your cause. Organizers of two such events share how to stage a successful murder mystery event:

Boyd County Public Library (Ashland, KY)

Amanda Clark, events coordinator at Boyd County Public Library (Ashland, KY), says the library uses murder mystery packets that are relatively inexpensive and available online. For example, Clark says, this year the library is using My Mystery Party (

.

The packet includes everything needed for a night of intrigue, including list of characters and instructions for the host. In this meet-and-mingle format, everyone who attends the event is a part of the show and receives information about his/her character before the event.

The drawback to this approach, Clark says, is that key characters might not show up for the event. She advises that organizations staging a murder mystery event for the first time start out small. "Pick a mystery that has a few parts, with no more than 20 to 30 people max."

Evergreen State Fairgrounds (Monroe, WA)

The Evergreen State Fairgrounds will hold its seventh murder mystery fundraiser this year to benefit food banks in Snohomish County, WA. The event uses eight to 10 characters portrayed by volunteers, staff members and a few professional actors. Audience members' participation is limited to putting together the clues as competing teams, determined by seating arrangements, to solve the mystery.

Bonnie Hausauer, who helps plan the event, says a key to a successful evening is to choose a mystery with a fun theme that people can dress up for, Hausauer says.

One idea that didn't work so well, Hausauer says, was having the mystery's characters mingle with the audience. This caused people to miss important clues, because not everyone talked to the same people. Now, characters give all clues onstage for the entire audience to hear.

Sources: Amanda Clark, Events Coordinator, Boyd County Public Library, Ashland, KY.
E-mail: Aclark@thebookplace.org
Bonnie Hausauer, Accounting Tech 2, Evergreen State Fairgrounds, Monroe, WA. E-mail: bj.hausauer@snoco.org

Fundraising for Libraries: How to Plan Profitable Special Events

Post-event Evaluation and Follow-up Actions

It is important to evaluate each of your library's special events as they progress and immediately following their completion. That thorough evaluation will help you decide whether to make it an annual event, to change it in certain ways or to drop it and move on to something else. Be sure to involve your event's patrons in the evaluation process.

Remember Your Work's Not Over Just Because the Party Is

To maximize your event's success, get to work as soon as possible after the event tying up loose ends. Here are some ways you can pitch in at the conclusion of a project or event:

1. As an event is taking place, make a pitch to several attendees to stick around for a few minutes to help where needed.

2. Take the lead in seeing that a project or event is evaluated within a week of its conclusion by key players — while it's still fresh in everyone's mind.

3. If certain individuals are responsible for follow-up procedures, confirm these tasks with them in writing in advance of event day.

4. Get personal hand-written notes of thanks promptly out to those who deserve them.

5. Return borrowed items the next day.

6. Be sure to celebrate the event's success with those who made it happen.

Plan Post-event Follow-up to Make Next Year Even Better

Evaluating both the successes and challenges of your annual fundraisers will never be easier than when the event is fresh in everyone's minds.

Plan to brainstorm within a week after the event to make sure good ideas won't be forgotten and solutions for things that might have been done differently won't slip through the cracks. Be sure to:

- **Plug post-event committee meetings into the event calendar.** Schedule this step at the same time you plot the timeline for the event itself. Volunteers will know to be available to provide input while information is fresh.

- **Provide digital voice recorders for key volunteers.** Lightweight and inexpensive, these handy devices even come on key chains, allowing people to make on-the-scene observations like "congestion at entrance" or "lots of great buzz about madrigal singers" that can be shared at event review.

- **Begin a blog on the event website.** Although encouraging anonymous feedback can result in mischief, it may also garner the unvarnished truth about why someone

will or won't attend again or recommend the event to friends. Screen comments before publishing in case names and privacy are compromised, but allow constructive criticism to be viewed by all.

- **Make courtesy calls to sponsors and benefactors.** Call them within a week to ask if they enjoyed the event and how they would streamline or expand the event's scope. They may have a business perspective different from most of your volunteers and committee members. This step also demonstrates how much you value their opinions in addition to financial support — particularly when they see their suggestions implemented in future events.

- **Consider improvements for next year.** If feedback about the facility, catering or atmosphere is lukewarm, immediately begin the search for possible alternatives. Watch for new hotel or business announcements, or cultivate new relationships with facilities or restaurant catering managers. Their specialty may be barbecue, but most facilities have the equipment and expertise to prepare any menu style.

Key Evaluation Questions

In evaluating your special events, large and small, come up with answers to the following key questions:

- Did it accomplish the goal (e.g., dollars raised or friends made or retained)?

- Was the mailing list broad enough? How could it be expanded next time?

- Were the costs low enough to make at least a 100 percent

profit (e.g., cost per person was $25 and you made $12.50 on each ticket)?

- Did the event's publicity benefit the organization? Whom did you contact? What coverage did you receive?

- Is interest/attendance in the event increasing or decreasing? If attendance is decreasing, why? How can you make the event more attractive, or at what point should it be replaced by a new event?

Use Survey Questions to Gather Attendee Feedback

Internal evaluation of special events is important, but continual improvement requires getting the thoughts and opinions of participants.

A participant survey included in information packets or left on chairs or tables can be a great way to go beyond the views of staff and volunteers, to gather novel and creative suggestions. Most event planners feel surveys work best when limited to a few key items, but the following list provides a variety of questions you might wish to include on your survey:

- What was your favorite or least favorite aspect of the event?
- If you could change one thing about the event, what would it be?
- What three words would you use to describe this event to a friend?
- Would you recommend this event to someone else? Why or why not?

- How did you hear about the event?
- How long ago did you plan to attend?
- Is this your first time attending one of our events?
- How would you rate the food, entertainment, venue, volunteers/workers, atmosphere, program?
- Is there anything that would have increased your enjoyment of this event?
- Was this event's ticket price too low, reasonable or too high?
- Would you have been willing to pay $X more to attend?
- What did you learn about our organization's mission/cause from tonight's event?
- Are you planning on attending next year's event? Why or why not?
- Would you be interested in volunteering in the future?
- Do you have any suggestions for improving the event next year?

Fourteen Internal Event Evaluation Questions

The tables have been stored, the funds counted and the final press release issued. Before taking a well-earned rest, be sure to conduct a post-event evaluation. Talking through an event's victories and challenges can identify areas of improvement and greatly facilitate next year's planning and preparation.

Some questions your evaluation might include are as follows:

1. How effectively did your event meet its primary goals and objectives?
2. How would you describe the event's planning and preparation? What went well and what could have gone better?
3. Did all members of the steering/planning committee participate in the planning process? Did members share responsibilities equally?
4. Was the event sufficiently promoted (through news releases, e-mail blasts, social media, posters, ads, fliers, etc.)? Did some communication channels seem more effective than others?
5. How did event attendance compare to expectations?

Were any demographics over- or under-represented?
6. To what extent were you able to track attendance and obtain contact information for attendees?
7. Were the decorations and environment appropriate for the event? What elements might be reused, and what elements will need to be changed?
8. Was the entertainment and food appropriate for the event? Did any problems arise in either area?
9. Were you satisfied with the performance of third-party vendors? Who will be used again, and who will not?
10. How would you rate the planning timeline? Did you have enough time to adequately plan and prepare?
11. Were revenue streams adequate to meet fundraising objectives?
12. Were there enough staff and volunteers to handle the event? Were they properly trained and overseen?
13. Was the event effectively structured and organized? Did activities transition smoothly from one to the next?
14. Were event-day roles and responsibilities clear? Were there any tasks that had too many or too few workers assigned to them?

Event Follow-up Ideas

What you do after an event is as important as what you do before.

Following your event, send photos to whomever you can recognize and include a brief note of appreciation.

In addition, put together a photo album for each sponsor that includes photos of guests, anything sponsor related, honorees, presenters and more. Use the photo album as your reason to meet with the sponsor, then make a point to get sponsor feedback during your meeting.

Wrap Up Your Event With a Press Release

You've done it all, from pre-planning to hosting to cleanup for your nonprofit's event, but don't forget one last detail — the wrap-up press release.

While you may feel like kicking back and enjoying the accolades of a job well done, the event is not complete until you send a wrap-up press release to the media, senior management, sponsors, volunteers and major participants.

Be sure the press release contains:

- Official name, date and number of attendees at the event.
- A heartfelt quote from the president or director of your library board about the importance of the event.
- Information about presentations made or awards given at the event and who gave those presentations or won the awards.
- Details of how funds were raised, how much was raised and what those funds will be used for, if applicable.
- Acknowledgement of major donors and sponsors of the event.
- Staff recognition and volunteer participation with a note of gratitude.
- Details about next year's event to entice readers to attend. If not all details are firm at the time of writing the wrap-up press release, offer information that is available, plus contact details so potential donors, sponsors or attendees can become involved next year.

To help issue your wrap-up press release in a timely manner, prepare a fill-in-the-blank format in advance, so you can simply plug in numbers and names, hit "send" and return to your post-event revelry.

Avoid Assumptions in Thanking Event Sponsors

Imagine you are organizing a large fundraising event. A local printing company gives a cash sponsorship and offers to provide free printing for all the event's promotional literature.

Sincerely grateful for this support, you warmly acknowledge these contributions at the event. Afterwards, the company's owner is very upset. "I did that printing as a special favor to you," he says. "Now I'm going to have every charity in town coming to ask me for free printing."

This scenario is based on events that actually happened, and which took significant effort to smooth over. The mistake is one anyone could make, but the lesson is clear: Never assume how event sponsors want to be thanked. Ask them!

Library Event Profile

Puzzle-filled Event Builds Excitement, Raises Funds

Puzzling over what kind of event might raise both friends and funds for your organization? Check out Silicon Valley Puzzle Day. Now in its fifth year, the annual event raises funds for the Morgan Hill Library Foundation (Morgan Hill, CA).

As for what types of games to share, Emily Shem-Tov, foundation president, says crossword puzzles seemed to be a good match for the library supporters. "We also decided to add sudoku into the mix because of our location and the number of math and computer science folks around that we thought would be interested," she says. Adding the popular number-based game led to a sponsorship/partnership with the American Institute of Mathematics (Palo Alto, CA).

Puzzle Day is actually two days of puzzle fun. Saturday is filled with workshops with prominent area puzzle experts, including sessions just for children. By including these experts, Shem-Tov says, "We've been able to attract some really wonderful presenters, including some of the top puzzle constructors and solvers in the country. Last year the Saturday and Sunday New York Times puzzles the weekend of the event were written by two of our speakers! It was amazing timing and a testament to the quality of our speakers."

Sunday is competition day, with tournaments for crosswords and su-doku plus bonus rounds of cryptic crosswords and killer sudoku. Tournaments for both adults and children draw entire families ready to compete with their peers.

Shem-Tov says that while the event itself doesn't bring in much money, "It definitely raises our profile in town, lets us get the word out about our organization and brings lots of new people into the library. Doing crosswords is usually a solitary activity done at one's kitchen table, so people really appreciate the opportunity to get to meet other people who share their passion."

Source: Emily Shem-Tov, President, Morgan Hill Library Foundation, Morgan Hill, CA.
E-mail: Emily@chocolatespoon.com

Promoting Your Niche Event

Planning a niche event similar to the Silicon Valley Puzzle Day presented by the Morgan Hill Library Foundation (Morgan Hill, CA)? Tap into persons enthusiastic about the niche area, says Emily Shem-Tov, foundation president.

"If you can tap into an existing passion and enthusiasm for your particular activity, those people can really help spread the word," she says.

Shem-Tov says that for the foundation's crossword puzzle/sudoku event, they post to online sites where crossword people go to play or to talk about writing or solving puzzles, and buy ads on Google and Facebook targeting people looking for puzzles.

Planning Next Year's Event

With another successful fundraising event behind you, and praise flowing from all directions, you may be wondering how to exceed attendees' expectations next year. You can begin laying the groundwork immediately with these steps.

✓ **Schedule a post-event meeting within a week.** Sometimes held in the form of a thank-you coffee or brunch, this event should have all committee members coming prepared with feedback about their specific areas. This helps identify and correct snags and record steps that worked splendidly and should be repeated.

✓ **Do a brief phone survey and thank-you call.** Contact key patrons and VIP guests to thank them for their support and ask them for their opinions about the event. Have four or five solid questions prepared so responses are consistently relevant from person to person. Ask if they mind your taking notes so they aren't bothered if you're clicking away on a keyboard as they answer (or think you're multi-tasking and not that interested in their reply).

✓ **Keep new venues on your radar.** A new hotel ballroom, banquet facility or convention center might be ready for use by next year. Would it be right for your next gala? Do they have in-house catering or food service? Stay on top of projected opening schedules, contact the newly hired banquet or facilities manager and be among the first to book if it fits your needs.

✓ **Solicit anonymous feedback.** Honest responses are all but guaranteed. Send a postage-paid survey card in your next mailing or post a survey on your website. A few key questions to use would include value for ticket price, length and content of program, quality of food and entertainment, and convenience of facilities.

✓ **Appoint a quality assurance manager.** Identify a conscientious committee member who can develop a detailed checklist of small things that make a big difference on the day of your event, including sparkling glassware, barrier-free entrances, tables in drafty areas and adequate supplies of tissue in restroom facilities that can be corrected before they become a problem.

Prestigious Award at the Heart of Westport Library Fundraiser

Westport Library (Westport, CT) presented award-winning director and screenwriter Barry Levinson with its annual Westport Library Award during its annual fundraiser on May 30.

Levinson won the Best Director Academy Award for Rain Man, starring Dustin Hoffman and Tom Cruise, and was nominated for 10 Oscars for directing and producing Bugsy. As a screenwriter, Levinson received Oscar nominations for ... And Justice for All, Diner and Avalon. Other Levinson productions include The Natural, Good Morning, Vietnam and Sleepers.

BOOKED for the evening is the library's trademarked signature fundraiser and has taken place for the past 14 years. At BOOKED for the evening, the library honors an individual whose work reflects the purpose of the library, which is to "nurture the love of learning and to enhance our understanding of the world." "The honoree is usually quite touched as the committee puts together a program that can be described as a mini Kennedy Center awards ceremony," said Cindy Clark, director of development for Westport Library. "We honor and highlight their life's body of work."

Planning for the event begins in September, with the event usually held sometime in May. The exact date is determined by the honoree's schedule.

The BOOKED for the evening committee consists of core members who have been in place since the beginning of the event concept, with new committee members added each year. The committee brainstorms honorees for the event. The criteria includes someone outstanding in his or her field whose work reflects the purpose of the library.

"As the committee brainstorms for the honoree, they also brainstorm for who has contacts to these individuals," Clark explained. "Based on the six degrees of separation theory, we usually are able to reach out to people through someone connected to the library."

Westport Library has several objectives with BOOKED for the evening. One is to entertain and enlighten the community. Another is to raise money for the library and let the community know that the library accepts donations.

"As one attendee remarked in an e-mail to us after the event, 'Your event last week was really excellent. I left informed, educated and entertained.' That sums up our goal quite nicely," Clark said. A fundraising goal is set each year depending on the needs of the library, and the library has been very successful in meeting these goals.

The town of Westport, which has a population of 26,000, funds approximately 80 percent of Westport Library's yearly budget; the balance is raised through fundraiser events and an annual appeal.

Source: Cindy Clark, Director of Development, Westport Library, Westport, CT. E-mail: cclark@westportlibrary.org

Lightning Source UK Ltd.
Milton Keynes UK
UKOW01f1159190713

214015UK00006B/221/P

9 781118 690499